Marriages

of

Norfolk County, VA.

1706-1792

-Volume #1 -

Compliled By:
Elizabeth Wingo

Southern Historical Press, Inc.
Greenville, South Carolina

This volume was reproduced from
an 1961 edition located in the
Publisher's private library
Greenville, South Carolina

**SOUTHERN HISTORICAL PRESS, INC.
PO BOX 1267
Greenville, SC   29601**

Originally printed & ©: Virginia 1961
Copyright Transferred 1983 to: Southern Historical Press, Inc
Reprinted By: Southern Historical Press, inc.
Greenville, SC   29601
ISBN #0-89308-401-8
Printed in the United States of America

Dedicated

to

My son Bruce Wingo
whose assistance in compiling this volume
was most helpful and companionable

also to

The Old Cannon Ball Society,
Children of the American Revolution,
whose members are a constant source of inspiration to me

INTRODUCTION

The Colony of Virginia was divided into eight shires or counties in 1634. Three years later, from that part of Elizabeth City County lying south of Hampton Roads, two new counties were formed; Upper County of New Norfolk and Lower County of New Norfolk.

The following is the earliest record pertaining to the Lower County of New Norfolk.

> "At a Court houlden in the Lower County of New Norfolk the
> 15th May 1637
> Present   Capt. Adam Thorowgood Esqr
>   Capt. John Sibsey
>   Mr. Edward Windham   Mr. Francis Mason
>   Mr. William Julian   Mr. Robert Came"

In 1691 Lower Norfolk County was divided into Norfolk County and Princess Anne County. The records of the present Norfolk County therefore start with the year 1637 and so are among the oldest in the nation. Princess Anne County records, prior to 1691, are found in the Norfolk County records. Descendants of those who settled here are scattered throughout the United States.

> "The First Court for Norfolk County, held after the Dividing Act, written in April 1691, was composed of the following gentlemen as Justices:
>
>   Colonel Lemuel Mason
>   Captain William Robinson
>   Captain John Hatton
>   Lieutenant Colonel Anthony Lawson
>   Captain William Craford
>   Major John Nichols
>   Mr. James Wilson"

It is regrettable that many of the earlier Marriage Bonds of Norfolk County fell prey to the vicissitudes of time and the Revolutionary War. During this War, records had to be moved in haste from the Courthouse to a private home for safety. It is probable that many of the loose Marriage Bonds (as well as other documents) were lost at that time. An entry in a Minute Book states some stored records were "destroyed by rats". On file in the Courthouse is an unsigned letter from a conscience stricken young man, returning the remaining few of some old documents, which he as a young boy had taken.

The Marriage Bonds of Norfolk County, prior to 1817, are not fully indexed.

The oldest Marriage Bond on file in Norfolk County, Virginia, reads as follows:

> Know all men by these presents that wee John Browne & Edward Browne both of Elizabeth river parish In ye County of Norfolk are bound and Stand Indebted unto ye wors'pfull (worshipful)

Thomas Hodgis in ye sume of one hundred pds Sterling to bee
paid by ye Sd (said) Thomas Hodgis, his heirs Exec'ts & Upon
demand to ye w'ch paym't will & truely to bee made & ------,
wee the above bounden doe bind us & (torn) of (torn) heirs etc
& either of ---- heirs Exec'ts adm'rs etc Joyntly & Severally
by these presents as Wittness our hands and Seals the 5th of
Oc'br 1706

The condition of this bond is Such that whereas this day John Browne hath
obtained license to Marry w'th Elizabeth Ivy both of ye parish & County
abovesd: Now if ye above bounden Edward Browne & John Browne or either of
y'm (them) or either of their heirs etc doe --- & keep --- --- the
abovesd Thomas Hodgis his heirs etc as alsoe all others granting ye Sd
License; that then this bond to be voyd or else to be in full force power
& Virtue.

                                                      John Browne
John Ferebee
James Wilson   Edw'd Browne

Mr. Lem Wilson, you may grant Jno. Browne a license to marry my daughter
Elizabeth Ivy, She having my consent thereunto & this Shall bee yee
Sufficient Warrant, given under my hand this 5th of x'br 1706.

                                                     Mary Ludgall

Note: Lemuel Wilson, son of Lt. Col. James Wilson, was Clerk of Norfolk
County Court in 1706.

Do not rely entirely on the spelling of names in these abstracts of Marriage
Bonds and "Minister's Returns". The Clerks (especially Deputy Clerks)
apparently at times failed to pay attention to the correct spelling of names,
for the spelling of the name of the groom on the bond is sometimes different
from his signature. When a groom had to sign his name by a mark (X), there
is no way of ascertaining the correct spelling of the surname. Oftimes a
groom wrote his name hastily (or was it nervousness?), making it quite
difficult to decipher.

You will sometimes find a discrepancy between the spelling of the name of the
bride on the bond and the signature of her father or guardian on the Consent.
Examples are: Etheridge - Etheredge, Balentine - Ballentine, Owens - Owins,
Hiley - Heley, et cetera.

Elizabeth (not Eliza) was often shortened to Eliza', and was sometimes
spelled Elisabeth.

Names ending in "t", often had the "t" doubled as Talbot - Talbott (or
Talbutt), Tart- Tartt, et cetera. Letters in some names were dropped, as
in Pulling - Pullin, and Wrighting - Wrightin (Writin). Some other differ-
ences were in Lovett - Lovitt, Deale, Deal or Dale, Tumblin - Tomblin, et
cetera.

My biggest concern was over spellings such as: Nicholos, Nichles, Nichols,

Nicols, Nicklis, Nicolos, Nickols and Nickels.

It is also apparent that a minister in making his "Returns" sometimes relied on his memory when recording dates of marriages as well as in his spelling of the names of the groom and bride. The "Ministers Returns" have been of great aid in this compilation as there are missing bonds. I must pay tribute to the late Mr. Richard Thomas (Tom) Whitehurst, historian, for his foresight in copying the "Returns" of Rev. Arthur Emmerson. His gift to me of his copies of these "Returns" has helped fill gaps in the bonds. Mr. Whitehurst had a genealogical turn of mind, quite accurate and factual. Any record provided by him is considered reliable. I am indeed indebted to him.

Mr. Edward Wilson James, historian, provided another source for bonds in his volumes of "The Lower Norfolk County Virginia Antiquary". Volume I was published in 1895.

I wish to thank Catherine Lindsay Knorr, who has published fourteen volumes of marriages, for her advice and encouragement. Without such, this volume may not have been compiled. I also wish to thank all those connected with the Norfolk County Clerk's Office for their cooperation - I am especially appreciative of the interest shown by Judge M. M. Hillard, former Clerk of Court, who permitted me to examine the marriage records.

Mrs. William B. Wingo
1230 Manchester Ave.
Norfolk 8, Va.

Had Henry Lord Maltravers followed through on a 1638 land grant, Norfolk County might have extended from the James River southward to Cape Hatteras.

These, roughly, were the north-south boundaries of a "county to be called Norfolk" given for development to Maltravers by the British crown through Sir John Harvey, governor of the Virginia colony.

Lord Maltravers was to "transport, settle and plant divers inhabitants" on the property. He never claimed the land, however, and the vast domain remained a paper one only.

But a county called Norfolk did come into existence and in its earliest stages comprised a considerable land mass although not quite as immense as that originally envisioned.

In the earliest days there was a Lower and Upper New Norfolk County. Both were formed from the much larger Elizabeth City County.

Upper Norfolk County in time became Nansemond County and Lower Norfolk County eventually was divided into the separate units of Norfolk and Princess Anne counties.

The area which is the Norfolk County of today was quick to play a role in the history of the nation. Within its boundaries was the Village of Great Bridge - an important link in the Virginia-North Carolina trade of the Revolutionary War period. Because of its geography, the village became the scene of the first important armed land clash of the Revolutionary War in the South. It proved to be a short battle won decisively by the American Patriots. It was this battle which started the downfall of Lord Dunmore in the Tidewater area and in the state.

The British received another setback in Norfolk County during the War of 1812. They attempted to gain control of the Elizabeth River but were repelled by withering fire from the county's Craney Island.

Territorially, the county played but a small role in the Civil War, but its men and units made their mark on many battle fronts. They were at Gettysburg, Cold Harbor, Seven Pines, The Crater and other scenes of conflict.

The area known as Lower Norfolk County was divided into Norfolk and Princess Anne counties in 1691. Simultaneously, the new Norfolk County made plans to move its judicial operations from the Lower Norfolk County Courthouse to a new building in the Town of Norfolk.

Court was conducted in Norfolk Town for about 100 years. The town became a borough, however, and the county people became dissatisfied because their courthouse was in territory over which they no longer had jurisdiction.

Consequently, the courthouse was moved in 1792 to nearby Washington Point where it remained until 1801 when it was moved to Portsmouth. It has remained in Portsmouth since, although not on the original site.

Norfolk County court records extend in an almost unbroken sequence from May 1, 1637, and are invaluable to those delving into the history of the state and of the nation.

The County is adjacent to three cities -- Norfolk, Portsmouth and South Norfolk. Each was born of county territory and each has expanded by annexing additional county territory.

It has been through the annexations, however, that the county has demonstrated its recuperative abilities and proven its mettle. It has almost always regained populations and revenues equal to those lost to the cities.

The principal crops of the county are corn and soybeans which it produces in abundance for domestic stores and export overseas. The county's potato farmers have long found their lands capable of supporting two crops annually. They operate on a rotating crop basis.

Building activity in the county has been brisk and, in 1960, averaged over $1,000,000 per month.

The county always has beckoned industry. Although many of the industries which located in the county have since been annexed, several still remain including shipyards, granaries, refineries, nurseries and lumber mills.

In 1950, the county launched a $28,000,000 school building program which has provided each county area with modern, fully-equipped structures for the education of future citizens.

The county school system is extremely progressive. It was the first of its area to install electronic language laboratories, to build campus-type school buildings, to install closed circuit classroom television and to experiment with teaching by automation.

With an eye to the future, the county currently is constructing a civic center at its village of history, Great Bridge. The center will place all of the county's governmental functions in new buildings grouped together in a central location.

Mike Evans

16 May 1761. Jacob ACWORTH and Susannah Hanaly, or Hansly. Sur.
Merick Meach.

14 October 1728. Solomon ADSHEAD and Charity Dison. Sur. George Hull.

7 April 1755. William ALEXANDER and Sarah Dupree. Sur. William
Alexander.

12 March 1774. William ALEXANDER and Mary Tracey. Sur. James Ballentine.

4 June 1785. Thomas ALLAN and Mary Murdoch. Sur. James Kincade. Thomas
and Mary both of Portsmouth, Virginia.

12 August 1792. John ALLINSON and Mary Ann Edwards. Sur. Samuel Livingston. Matthew Bunbury, guardian of Mary Ann consents for her. Wit.
William Johnson and John Williams.

24 December 1781. Edmund ALLMAND and Nancy Smallwood. Sur. Caleb Herbert.

10 August 1769. Edmond ALLMON and Lucretia Braithwait. Sur. Edward
Mitchell. Wit. Samuel Boush. John Seldon consents for Edmond; no relationship stated. Note: Bond written Allmon, signature Allmond, or Allmand.

25 January 1785. Joseph ANATOIER and Betty Whitehurst, dau. of John Whitehurst, deceased. Sur. John Whitehurst.

7 July 1785. James ANDERSON and Cherry Ritter. Married by Rev. Edward
Mintz.

6 January 1785. Joseph ANDRE and Mary Wright. Sur. Bernard Magnien.

3 January 1775. Robert ANDREWS and Eliza Ballard. Sur. Will Ballard.

1 July 1761. Thomas APPLEWHAITE and Mary Archer. Sur. Edward Archer.

23 September 1761. James ARCHDEACON and Parnell Ingham. Sur. George
Chamberlaine.

11 August 1733. Edward ARCHER and Mrs. Mary Anguish. Sur. John Hutchings.

5 September 1761. Edward ARCHER and Dinah Belgrove. Sur. Nicholas Wonycutt.

19 July 1787. John ARCHER and Elizabeth Jones. Married by Rev. Walker Maury.

2 February 1764. John ARDIS and Mrs. Louisa Taylor. Sur. John Woodsid (e).

2 February 1785. James ARLINGTON and Elizabeth Shepherd. Sur. William Crocker.

25 November 1769. Freer ARMSTON and Elizabeth Gardner. Sur. Griffin Peart.

20 October 1787. John ARMSTRONG and Rebecca Hopkins. Married by Rev. Needler Robinson.

20 April 1765. Robert ARMSTRONG and Jamima Ballentine. Sur. Solomon Vester.

2 October 1773. Thomas ARNAT and Sarah Steel. Sur. Wright Brickell. Sarah, born 3 October 1751, is the daughter of Sarah Steel. Ref: The Lower Norfolk County Virginia Antiquary.

1 November 1752. James ASHLEY and Mrs. Eliza Langley. Sur. William Ivy.

29 July 1762. James ASHLEY and Mary Calvert, dau. of Lucy Pugh who consents for her. Sur. John Woodsid (e).

28 July 1724. John ASHLEY and Mrs. Eliza Godfrey. Sur. John Wishard. Wit. Charles Portlock. John is of Princess Anne County, Virginia.

28 April 1763. John ASHLEY and Margarett Williamson. Sur. John Williamson.

16 April 1790. Henry AUSTIN and Jennet Jack. Married by Rev. Arthur Emmerson.

17 November 1727. James AVERY and Mary McNary. Sur. Solomon Wilson.

29 July 1731. James AVERY and Frances Brett. Sur. J. Phripp.

3 November 1773. William AYLES and Eliza Hudson. Sur. Henry Bressie.

21 July 1771. Bernard BABB and Jane Steel, dau. of John Steel. Sur. Wright Brickell. Ref: The Lower Norfolk County Virginia Antiquary.

4 March 1784. Richard BACON and Mrs. Joyce Wallace. Sur. Aaron Pullen.

8 April 1758. Samuel BACON and Mary Ann Dale. Sur. Peter Dale.

18 September 1789. Daniel BAILEY and Sarah Deveo. Sur. John Cooke.

10 September 1777. William BAILEY and Mary Taylor. Sur. Thomas Ellis.

7 December 1784. William Armistead BAILEY and Sarah Ramsay. Sur. James Taylor.

26 December 1789. William BAINE and Catherine Alwinkle, orphan of Isaac Alwinkle. Sur. John Britton. Married 17 January 1790 by Rev. Arthur Emmerson.

1790 or 1791. David BAKER and Judith Johnson. Married by Rev. Arthur Emmerson.

5 September 1768. John BAKER and Sarah Jackson. Sur. Stephen Tankard.

3 April 1780. Thomas BAKER and Mary Herriter. Sur. Moody Barham.

26 May 1744. William BAKER and Rebecca Joel. Sur. Samuel Boush.

20 August 1778. David BALLANCE and Frances Bartee. Sur. Thomas Jacobs.

17 April 1777. Richard BALLANCE and Mrs. Ann Prescott. Sur. Malachi Wilk(torn).

16 September 1772. James BALLENTINE and Ann Hubbard. Sur. William Skinker.

6 January 1779. James BALLENTINE and Sarah Denby. Sur. Richard Grant.

11 October 1785. James BALLENTINE and Frances Valentine. Sur. Joshua Ballentine. John Herbert makes oath that Frances is of lawful age.

9 April 1789. John BALLENTINE and Mrs. Sarah Manning. Sur. John Brooks.

16 November 1736. Paul BALLENTINE and Ann Cawson. Sur. Robert Todd.

18 October 1779. William BALLENTINE and Hannah Rudder. Sur. Thomas Jacobs.

5 September 1767. Robert BANKS and Mrs. Sarah Symonds. Sur. Matt Kelly.

13 May 1754. William BANKS and Mary Collart. Sur. Archibald Williamson.

26 October 1765. Benjamin BANNERMAN and Mrs. Margaret Streep. Sur. Christopher Thompson.

1 February 1770. Aaron BARBER and Elizabeth Maund, who consents for self. Sur. John Southerland.

5 September 1782. Willis BARBER and Mary Ferebee. Sur. Thomas Bressie.

30 April 1787. Anthony BARDY and Mrs. Mary Consaul. Sur. O. Mard. Married by Rev. Arthur Emmerson.

19 December 1791. John BARNES and Kezia Hoffler. Thomas Hoffler, brother of Kezia, makes oath Kezia is of lawful age and he is surety.

3 July 1778. Richard BARR and Elizabeth Burnett, dau. of Mary Burnett. Sur. Charles Randolph. Ref: The Lower Norfolk County Virginia Antiquary.

21 December 1791. George BARRETT and Mrs. Mary James, dau. of Thomas Lowrey, who consents for her. Sur. John Foster.

23 January 1772. Jonathan BARRETT and Amy Lowe. Sur. Philip Carbery. Ann Williams makes oath that Amy is of lawful age.

10 August 1770. Robert BARRON and Susanna Loyall. Sur. Paul Loyall.

1 December 1780. Andre BARTEE and Nancy Boushell, dau. of William Boushall. Sur. Daniel Cutherell. Andre is son of John Bartee. Ref: The Lower Norfolk County Virginia Antiquary.

23 December 1791. James BARTEE and Sarah Gamewell. Sur. Richard Thelaball.

5 October 1779. Samuel BARTEE and Peggy Mason, dau. of William Mason, who consents for her. Sur. William Warren. Wit. Moses Langley.

4 September 1773. Richard BASSETT and Elizabeth Moore. Sur. James Bird.

9 December 1777. William BATCHELOR and Mary Harper, dau. of Mary Harper, Sr., who consents for her. Sur. John Braidfoot.

24 December (?) 1786. Caleb BATING and Sarah Butt, married by Rev. Needler Robinson.

17 May 1782. John BAXTOR and Mary Jones, dau. of Benjamin Jones. Sur. James Leitch.

24 December 1771. Thomas BAYLEY and Rebecca Harmmon. Sur. William Bayley.

28 April 1713. Waltor BAYLEY and Mary Etheredge. Sur. William Dale, Sr.

?? 1735 Alexander BAYNE and Margaret Connor. Sur. Anthony Conner.

2 November 1792. James BAYNE and Dicay Dunderwin. Sur. Thomas Crafts. James makes oath he is of lawful age. Married 3 November by Rev. Arthur Emmerson.

31 January 1769. John BAYNE and Molley Ashley. Sur. George Webb. Lydia Christian consents for Molly, dau. of William and Lydia Ashley and makes oath that she is of lawful age. No relationship is stated.

4 January 1773. John BAYNE and Mary Wishart, of Princess Anne County. Sur. Samuel Boush. William Wishart consents for his sister Mary.

18 January 1753. Martain BAYNE and Sarah Southerlin, dau. of David Southerlin, who consents for her. Sur. Alexander Bayne. Wit. John Southerland.

11 October 1792. John BEGG and Sarah Poole, dau. of Howard Pool. Nathaniel Murphy, surety, makes oath Sarah is of lawful age.

7 January 1779. John BELL and Biar Shipwash, dau. of Ambrose Shipwash, who consents for her. Sur. Willis Shipwash. Wit. Caleb Hanbury and William Shipwash.

30 May 1722. William BELL and Ellenor Corprew. Sur. Solomon Wilson. Wit. Tabitha Wilson.

? December 1728. Edward BEMBOWE and Eliza Falioner. Sur. Solomon Wilson.

22 November 1791. Spencer BENNETT and Lucy Morris. Sur. John Morris. Spencer makes oath he is of lawful age. Married 5 January 1792 by Rev. Arthur Emmerson.

29 December 1790. William BENTHALL and Elisabeth Perkins. Sur. John Perkins.

28 June 1783. John BESSOM and Elizabeth Williams, dau. of Elizabeth Starr, who consents for her. Sur. Samuel Blews.

2 April 1779. John BEST and Sarah Hobbs. Sur. Thomas Best.

13 November 1792. William BEST and Anne Grimes, orphan of John Grimes. William Powell, surety, makes oath Anne is of lawful age.

13 February 1741/2. George BEVEN and Ms. Merion Godfrey. Sur. John Cooke. Wit. John Denby and Thomas Newton.

20 December 1761. Robert BIGNALL and Peggy Parrish. Sur. W. R. Curle.

2 May 1763. James BIRD and Dianna Saunders. Sur. John Wheatly.

3 October 1778. George BISCOE and Elizabeth Talbot. Sur. William Ingram.

27 February 1779. John BIVENS and Mary Peyton. Sur. John Pool.

21 May 1771. James BLAIR and Catherine Eustace. Sur. Archibald Campbell.

27 April 1789. James BLAMEN and Elisabeth Hutchings. Sur. John Savage Calvert.

11 April 1790. Richard BLOXON and Mary Taylor. Married by Rev. Arthur Emmerson.

12 February 1785. Benjamin BLYTHE and Mrs. Mary Dougle. Sur. Jeremiah Nelson Chandler. Wit. Benjamin Putnam.

16 December 1790. Bennet BOGGESS and Elizabeth Kelso. Sur. Hillary Butt. Bennet makes oath that Elizabeth is of lawful age.

30 January 1773. John BOGGESS to Mary Ann Thelaball. Sur. Joshua Williamson.

12 January 1791. Benjamin BOULTON and Mrs. Fanny Bunting. Sur. Noah Coffield.

16 April 1784. William BOULTON and Mrs. Elizabeth Bruce. Sur. Samuel Ives. Married 1 May 1784 by Rev. Edward Mintz.

8 September 1787. Dr. Michael BOURK and Mrs. Frances Langley. Sur. Simon Varshon. Married 10 September by Rev. Walker Maury.

8 February 1763. Arthur BOUSH and Ann Sweny, dau. of Charles Sweny of Sewells Point, who consents for her. Sur. Francis Wishart. Wit. Christopher Calvert and Peggy Calvert.

6 May 1774. Charles Sayer BOUSH and Martha Sweny. Sur. Thomas Claiborne.

25 January 1759. Goodrich BOUSH and Mary Wilson. Sur. William Bradley.

10 January 1787. John BOUSH and Frances Moseley Mumford. Sur. Augustine Tabb. Married 11 January 1787 by Rev. Walker Maury.

18 June 1777. Nathaniel BOUSH and Ann Willoughby. Sur. John Willoughby.

21 July 1779. Nathaniel BOUSH and Mary Tabb. Sur. John Tabb.

1 July 1783. Nathaniel BOUSH and Ann Hudson. Sur. Robert Boush.

4 September 1787. Nathaniel BOUSH and Mrs. Elizabeth Tabb. Sur. Augustine Tabb. Married 4 September by Rev. Walker Maury.

31 October 1784. Robert BOUSH and Catherine Ballard. Sur. William King B - - - - (torn off).

21 May 1783. William BOUSH and Margaret Taylor. Sur. James Taylor.

29 February 1788. James BOUSHEL and Mary Nash. Married by Rev. Needler Robinson.

20 October 1778. James BOUSHELL and Lydia Bascome. Sur. Arthur Denby.

19 May 1785. James BOUSHELL and Mrs. Christian Dorvey. Sur. William Boushell, Sr.

23 July 1785. William BOUSHELL, Jr. and Latitia Taylor. Sur. Uphaney Boushell.

18 April 1778. Preeson BOWDOIN and Courtney Tucker. Sur. Robert Tucker.

14 December 1789. Preeson BOWDOIN, Jr., and Rebecca Bacon, dau. of Samuel Bacon, who consents for her. Sur. Benjamin Jordon.

5 October 1785. Willis BOWERS and Frances Ellis whose guardian, Willis Culpepper consents for her; no relationship stated. Wit. John Bowers. Sur. Spieavy Wyatt.

11 April 1759. Malcom BOWIE and Barbara Munro. Sur. Francis Miller.

9 August 1791. Corbin BRACKET and Elizabeth Holdness. Thomas Holdness, brother of Elizabeth, makes oath she is of lawful age and he is surety. Married 10 August by Rev. Arthur Emmerson.

21 January 1750. William BRADLEY and Mrs. Mary Wilson. Sur. Samuel Boush, Jr.

28 March 1789. Henry BRAGG and Diane Wythe Talbot, orphan of Thomas Talbot. Wit. Cornelius Calvert, Sr. Sur. John Brent.

12 March 1773. John BRAIDFOOT and Blandinah Moseley. Sur. Richard Taylor.

12 December 1764. George BRAITHWAITE and Lucretia Williams. Sur. John Phripp, Sr.

9 June 1732. Robert BRAMBLE and Mary Ewel. Sur. Cornelius Calvert.

17 March 1753. Willis BRAMBLE and Mary Ashley. Sur. William Ashley.

3 August 1778. John BRANON and Mrs. Mary Burnet. Sur. Richard Barr.

4 February 1782. John BRANON and Mary Walker. Sur. Paul Watlington.

13 March 1785. John BRANON and Ann Lush, whose guardian consents for her. Sur. George Callis. Note: Guardian unnamed.

9 April 1764. Irby BRESSIE and Ann Ivy. Sur. Samuel Bressie. Wit. Daniel Sanford.

21 June 1787. James BRESSIE and Martha Shipwash. Sur. John Armstrong.

15 July 1769. Samuel BRESSIE and Sarah Murden. Sur. William Bressie.

31 May 1783. Robert BRETT and Margaret Madden. Sur. Richard Coleman.

21 January 1769. William BRETT and Rebecca Jacobs. Sur. James Murphree.

7 October 1775. John BRICKELL, Jr., and Eliza Hudson. Sur. George Rae.

27 March 1772. Mathias BRICKELL and Mrs. Lydia Hodges. Sur. Henry Fleming.

2 March 1770. Wright BRICKELL and Elizabeth Steel, dau. of John Steel, who consents for her. Sur. John Ardis. Wit. Frances Johnson.

16 November 1771. Captain Bristol BROWN and Sarah Cann. Sur. Paul Proby.

24 April 1782. John BRITTEN and Margaret McDurman. Sur. Demse Viel(Veal).

5 May 1789. William BRITTON and Susanah Alwincle. Sur. Paul D. Luke. Michael Warren makes oath that Susanah is of lawful age; no relationship stated. Married 23 May by Rev. Arthur Emmerson.

26 May 1792. William BRITTON and Lydia Bunting, orphan of Benjamin Bunting. Sur. Lyon Culpeper.

28 August 1790. William BROAD and Mrs. Susanna Bell. Sur. John Waterman.

17 July 1782. Ludowick BROADIE and Mary Whiddon. Sur. William Cunningham.

16 December 1784. John BROOKES and Sarah Butt. Sur. Lemuel Butt.

8 October 1782. Robert BROUGH and Betsy Bradley. Sur. Paul Proby.

1 June 1762. Captain Hugh BROWN and Rhodah Morgan. Sur. Hardess Lamount.

22 May 1764. James BROWN and Mrs. Mary Walker. Sur. James Smith.

1 September 1790. James BROWN and Polly Ritter, dau. of Henry Ritter. Philip Ritter, guardian of Polly, consents for her and is surety.

23 November 1791. James BROWN and Mrs. Margaret Bell. Sur. William Brown.

17 September 1756. John BROWN and Mary Heley. Sur. Edward Hiley.

30 April 1767. John BROWN and Sally Walke, dau. of Anne Walke, who consents for her and states she "was 22 years of age of 22 of July last". Sur. Robert Crooks.

31 March 1789. Captain John BROWN, Sr., and Frances Day of Isle of Wight Co. Sur. John Patterson. Lewis Day, brother, consents for Frances. Wit. Thomas Peirce. Married 31 March 1789 by Rev. Arthur Emmerson.

10 December 1751. Joseph BROWN and Catherine Edmonds, dau. of Mary Prichard, who consents for her. Sur. Jonathan Porter. Wit. Joseph Lipscomb.

23 November 1791. Joseph BROWN and Juda Mott. William Brown, surety, makes oath Joseph is of lawful age.

26 March 1792. Joshua BROWN and Mary Tart. Sur. Thomas Tart.

17 September 1791. Samuel BROWN and Mrs. Sabra Dickson. Sur. James Harper.

13 April 1789. Solomon BROWN and Nancy Makins. Stephen Makins, brother of Nancy, consents for her and is surety. Married 26 April 1789 by Rev. Arthur Emmerson.

13 May 1769. William BROWN and Mary Smithson, widow of William Smithson and dau. of Lemuel Coverly, who consents for her. Sur. Thomas Price.

28 October 1790. William BROWN and Mrs. Charlotte Gilmour. Sur. Neil Fullarton. Married 29 October 1790 by Rev. Arthur Emmerson.

5 October 1706. John BROWNE and Elizabeth Ivy, dau. of Mary Ludgall, who consents for her. Sur. Edward Browne. Wit. John Ferebee and James Wilson.

14 September 1792. Absolom BRUCE and Hannah Smith, orphan of John Smith. Malachi Bruce, surety, makes oath Hannah is of lawful age. Married 20 September by Rev. Arthur Emmerson.

13 February 1762. Alexander BRUCE and Mrs. Elizabeth Curle. Sur. Richard Scott.

17 November 1785. Archibald BRUCE and ----- Best. Sur. William Moore Bruce.

3 April 1792. Archibald BRUCE and Mrs. Sarah Wildair. Sur. William Rhonnald.

11 June 1783. John BRUCE and Priciller Owens. Sur. Samuel Hatton. Ref: The Lower Norfolk County Virginia Antiquary.

23 August 1783. William Moore BRUCE and Mrs. Mary Bailey. Joshua Miars, guardian of William, consents for him and states he is underage.

18 January 1791. George BRUMFIELD and Mrs. Ann Donnell. Sur. John Nickles. Note: Bond written Bromfield and Nickols, signatures Brumfield and Nickles.

4 July 1738. James O. BRYAN (or O'Bryan) and Mary Langley. Sur. John Langley.

22 March 1791. Thomas BRYAN and Lydia Boulton. Sur. Benjamin Bolton.

17 December 1790. William BUD and Nancy Guy. Sur. John Guy.

25 September 1789. William BULLY and Cortney Ketor, dau. of John Ketor, who consents for her. Sur. John Western. Wit. Solomon Taylor, Willoughby Machart (Marchant?).

5 May 1785. Joseph BUMOTHE and Mrs. Ann Gordon. Sur. John Fulchiron. Note: Bond written Bumothe, signature Bermothe.

5 August 1790. Mathew BUNBURY and Mary Clarkson. Married by Rev. Arthur Emmerson.

6 December 1768. Benjamin BUNTING and Letta Lewelling. Sur. Joseph Hutchings. Robert Fry, Clerk of Vestry, makes oath that Letta, the dau. of Edward and Margaret Lewelling, was born 24 October 1747.

_____ December 1787. William BUNTING and Mrs. Jennett Owins. Sur. Edward Herbert.

23 December 1777. George Wright BURGES and Mrs. Aphia Ives. Sur. Malachi Burges.

29 December 1760. Thomas BURGES and Amy White. Sur. Patrick White.

27 May 1784. John BURGESS and Ann Ferrol. Sur. Thomas Morris.

12 July 1787. John BURGESS and Elizabeth Goosburg. Married by Rev. Walker Maury.

31 March 1779. Nathaniel BURGESS, Jr., and Mary Burgess, dau. of Nathaniel Burgess, who consents for her. Sur. Thomas Burgess.

? June 1711. George BURGIS and Mary Butt. Sur. Richard Butt. Wit. Lemuel Wilson and Thomas Butt.

19 June 1787. Richard BURKE and Mrs. Margaret McGuire. Sur. John Brannon, Jr.

28 March 1770. Thomas BURKE and Mary Freeman, dau. of William Freeman, who consents for her and states she is underage. Sur. James Gilchrist. Wit. Frances McKerall.

10 April 1779. Robert BURLEY and Mary Holstead, dau. of James Holstead, who consents for her. Sur. Reuben Wiles. Wit. Ehitet(?) Whitehurst.

21 June 1755. Thomas BUSHELL and Max(?) Murden. Sur. John Corprew.

14 March 1767. Charles BUSHNELL and Catherine McGee. Sur. Thomas Clark. Ref: The Lower Norfolk County Virginia Antiquary.

13 January 1763. Christopher BUSTIN and Elizabeth Dunn. Sur. Lewis Hansford. John Dunn and Nicholas Poole make oath that Elizabeth is of lawful age.

18 April 1763. Charles BUTLER and Jane Dison. Sur. William Harvy.

8 October 1792. Matthew BUTLER and Kez--- Butt. Sur. Wm. G. Knight.

13 September 1766. Arthur BUTT and Martha Riddlehurst, dau. of Anne Riddlehurst, who makes oath Martha is of lawful age. Sur. Thomas Butt. Wit. Ann Butt and John Butt.

3 December 1792. Benjamin BUTT and Mrs. Mary Holstead. Sur. Jeremiah Butt.

28 December 1785. Isaiah BUTT and Mary Holstead. Sur. Matthew Holstead.

22 June 1791. Henry BUTT and Sally Holstead, dau. of Simon Holstead. Benjamin Butt, surety, makes oath Sally is of lawful age.

27 December 1790. James BUTT and Fanny Herbert, dau. of John Herbert, who consents for her. Sur. William Herbert. Wit. William Herbert and Arthur Herbert.

29 July 1765. John Butt and Elizabeth Fairfield. Sur. Thomas Butt.

12 January 1744. Josiah BUTT and Mary Boush. Willis Wilson, Jr., guardian of Mary, consents for her and is surety.

14 August 1772. Malaba BUTT and Eliza Bartee, dau. of William Bartee. Sur. Thomas Bartee. Ref: The Lower Norfolk County of Virginia Antiquary.

27 February 1790. Nathaniel BUTT and Mrs. Frances Hall. Sur. Wilson Butt.

13 June 1715. Richard BUTT and Dina (h) Butt. Sur. Robert Butt. Wit. Thomas Butt, William Butt and Thomas Butt.

23 ---- ----. Richard BUTT and Frances _____. (mutilated).

5 August 1784. Willis BUTT and Mrs. Penelope McCoy. Sur. Joshua McCoy, Sr.

10 December 1792. Wilson BUTT, Jr. and Elizabeth Happer. Sur. John Armstrong, Jr.

5 December 1789. William CADENHEAD and Sarah Jolliff. Sur. James Gillcott. James Jolliff makes oath that Sarah is of lawful age and the orphan of James Jolliff; no relationship is stated. Married by Rev. Arthur Emmerson 5 December 1789.

4 June 1791. Richard CAIN and Ann Boushell, orphan of James Boushell. Sur. Armiger Webb. Ann makes oath she is of lawful age.

14 September 1791. James CALLAHAN and Celia Smith, orphan of Thomas Smith. John Cowper, surety, makes oath Celia is of lawful age.

25 June 1789. George CALLIS and Mary Miller. Sur. William Boushell. Caleb Miller, brother of Mary, consents for her. Wit. Benjamin Miller and Kedar Webb.

1 May 1770. William CALLIS and Hannah Dale. Sur. George Collins.

27 October 1762. Christopher CALVERT and Peggy Boush. Sur. Arthur Boush.

5 May 1772. Cornelius CALVERT and Eliza' Thruston. Sur. George Gordon.

2 May 1783. Jonathan CALVERT and Elizabeth Newton. Sur. William Boush.

28 July 1744. Captain Maximilian CALVERT and Mrs. Mary Savage. Sur. Cornelius Calvert. John Hutchings consents for Mary Savage; no relationship stated. Wit. Goodrich Boush and Nicholas Wonycott.

3 July 1764. Samuel CALVERT and Peggy Ross. Sur. Alexander Gordon. W. R. Curle of Elizabeth City County, guardian of Samuel, consents for him and states he is the son of Cornelius Calvert, deceased. Wit. Nicholas Powell and Robert Bright.

6 April 1789. Samuel CALVERT and Mary Moseley. Sur. Jonathan Calvert.

13 January 1757. Saunders CALVERT and Frances Tucker. Sur. John Tucker.

15 July 1760. William CALVERT and Ann Barlow. Sur. Goodrich Boush.

15 May 1787. Angus CAMERON and Mrs. Margaret Brown. Sur. Archibald McGoun.

12 March 1784. George CAMERON and Mary Bailey. Sur. George Mills. Ann Wilson, sister-in-law of Mary, makes oath that she is of lawful age and that her father is dead.

22 January 1767. Duncan CAMPBELL and Ann Wha_____ (blotted out). Sur. Nicholas Winterton.

21 June 1784. Joseph CAMPBELL and Sarah Dunn, whose guardian (not named) consents for her. Sur. John Fleet.

16 April 1784. James CANN and Margaret Veale. Sur. Samuel Veale. Samuel Veale is guardian of Margaret; no relationship stated.

21 September 1785. James CANN and Sally Veale. Sur. Thomas Veale.

7 January 1791. James CANNON and Jane Walker. Sur. William Langister. Jane makes oath she is of lawful age.

24 March 1789. George CAPRON and Elizabeth Silvester. Edmund Allmand makes oath that Elizabeth is of lawful age and the orphan of Richard Silvester, deceased.

2 September 1762. Philip CARBERY and Sarah Galt. Sur. Richard Scott.

18 January 1791. Charles CARLINE and Isabella Moore. Sur. John Hamilton.

29 November 1791. Barnaby CARNEY and Ann Hodgis, dau. of William Hodgis, Sr., who consents for her. Sur. James Carney. Wit. Richard Silvester.

13 January 1792. James CARNEY and Charlotte Eastwood. Thomas Powell, surety, makes oath Charlotte is of lawful age.

21 February 1772. John CARNEY and Frances Sparrow. Sur. Peter Sparrow.

3 August 1774. Richard CARNEY, Jr., and Sally Lewelling. Sur. Richard Carney. Demse Veal, guardian of Sally, consents for her.

14 March 1792. Thomas CARNEY and Sarah Grimes. Sur. John Taylor.

1 July 1783. Wright CARNEY and Sarah Hodges. Sur. Solomon Tatem. Joshua Miars, guardian of Sarah, consents for her and makes oath she is above 18 years of age.

-- ---- 1787. James CARROL and Catherine Powell? Note: Only a fragment of this bond left.

8 February 1782. Thomas CARROLL and Elizabeth Nicols. Sur. Susanne Nichols.

28 November 1785. Martin Sam CARSON and Mary Harris. Sur. Samuel Harris.

12 October 1791. Robert CARSON and Jemina Butt. Sur. Samuel Butt.

-- ---- 1787. Lemuel CARTER and Frances Price. Married by Rev. Walker Maury.

10 May 1761. Thomas CARTER and Mary Carter, dau. of Joseph Carter, who consents for her. Wit. Zackariah Hutchings and John Lewelling.

10 August 1790. William CARTER and Ann Culpeper. Zadoch Carter, surety, makes oath that Ann, the orphan of William Carter, is of lawful age. Married 11 August 1790 by Rev. Arthur Emmerson.

10 August 1790. Zadoch CARTER and Mrs. Polly Cherry. Sur. William Carter. Married 11 August 1790 by Rev. Arthur Emmerson.

5 December 1772. Thomas CARTWRIGHT and Mrs. Susanah Esther. Sur. John Braidfoot.

19 September 1789. Demsev CASSEY and Elizabeth Crofts, dau. of Thomas Crofts, who consents for her. Sur. John Moore. Wit. George Wainwright.

23 October 1768. John CAVENDER and Elizabeth Franks, dau. of Robert Franks, who consents for her. Sur. Henry Crosby and Andrew Willson. Note: Bond written Cavender, signature probably Cavendor.

14 September 1768. Robert CAWSON and Lydia Herbert. Sur. Henry Herbert.

20 December 1770. James CHAMPION and Rebecca Stackpole. Sur. Bartholomew Thompson. Wit. Richard Evers Lee.

2 May 1783. Jeremiah Nelson CHANDLER and Mrs. Susannah McDonald. Sur. Thomas Simpson.

20 May 1769. David CHAPMAN and Mrs. Courtney Lowrey. Sur. John Pearson.

4 June 1789. Ralph CHAPMAN and Jane Brown. David Leitch, surety, makes oath that Jane, orphan of William Brown, is of lawful age.

14 May 1791. Alexander CHERRY and Sophia Willie. Warrington Stevens, surety, makes oath Sophia is of lawful age. Married 18 May by Rev. Arthur Emmerson.

22 May 1787. Hillary CHERRY and Anna Brown. Sur. Abel Brown.

23 December 1790. Isaiah CHERRY and Lydia Moore. Married by Rev. Arthur Emmerson.

11 January 1789. James CHERRY and Sarah Everage. Sur. Samuel McPherson. James Cherry makes oath that Sarah is of lawful age.

9 December 1782. Jeremiah CHERRY and Mary Owens. Sur. William Owens.

9 March 1792. Mackse (Maxey) CHERRY and Lydia Deale. Married 29 March by Rev. Arthur Emmerson.

16 September 1790. Peter CHERRY and Mary Godfrey. Benjamin Kinder, surety, makes oath that Mary, orphan of Matthew Godfrey, is of lawful age.

25 November 1790. Thomas CHERRY and Mary Moore. Married by Rev. Arthur Emmerson.

10 September 1761. Richard CHESHIRE and Dinah Miller. Sur. Nicholas Wonycott.

16 August 1759. John CHESHIRE and Mary Miller. Sur. Matthew Godfrey.

19 January 1758. William CHISHOLM and Sarah Kinner. Sur. William Orange.

12 June 1754. Matthias CHRISTIAN and Lydia Ashley. Sur. Thomas Roberts.

25 October 1753. Joseph CHURCH and Sarah Wilson. Sur. John Hamilton.

13 April 1759. Thomas CLAIBORNE and Uphan Sweny, dau. of Charles Sweny of Sewells Point, who consents for her. Sur. Daniel Sweny.

15 July 1784. Thomas CLARKSON and Mary Veale. Sur. Thomas Veale.

11 March 1754. John CLEEVES and Ann Silvester, dau. of Richard William Silvester, who consents for her. Sur. Thomas Jones. Wit. Dokis Weston and Joseph Weston.

19 July 1785. Daniel CLEMENTS and Elisabeth Moore. Sur. John Moore.

8 January 1787. Benjamin COAKLEY and Sarah Dale. Sur. William Stokes.

15 October 1768. Demcey COFFIELD and Westcoat Carney. Sur. Richard Carney.

9 February 1792. Noah COFFIELD and Martha Smith, orphan of John Smith. Wilson Smith, surety, makes oath his ward, Martha, is of lawful age; no relationship stated.

21 May 1770. Slaughter COFIELD and Mary Carney. Sur. Richard Carney.

10 August 1785. Samuel COLBOUN and Amelia Minner. Sur. John Fulchiron. Note: Bond written Colboun, signature Colborn.

8 February 1769. John COLES and Rebecca Tucker. Sur. Henry Tucker.

20 January 1763. Saunders COLLEY and Mrs. Honour McCloud. Sur. John Dunn. Note: Bond written Saunders, signature Sanders.

26 June 1742. George COLLINS and Mrs. Mary Phillips. Sur. Richard Taylor.

2 July 1778. George COLLINS and Mrs. Anne Lewelling. Sur. Ferebee Hodges.

6 December 1779. George COLLINS and Mrs. Sarah Callis. Sur. Maxy Grimes.

1 June 1785. Henry COLLINS and Mrs. Martha Jones. Sur. Nathaniel Murphy.

13 December 1789. Henry COLLINS and Ann Bland. Sur. Thomas Bland. Married by Rev. Arthur Emmerson.

16 December 1767. John COLLINS and Frances Jones. Sur. Richard Jones.

23 December 1773. John COLLINS and Mrs. Dinah Dale. Sur. John Boush.

1 February 1780. John COLLINS and Mary Ann Edwards. Sur. Thomas Edwards.

19 April 1791. Edmund COLONEY and Joice Redd. Sur. John Redd.

14 June 1787. Matthew COLVERT and Hannah Tennis, dau. of Joseph Tennis, who consents for her. Sur. Thomas Best. Wit. Matthew Farthere and Danil Burch.

28 March 1792. Charles CONE and Susannah Addison, orphan of Littleton Addison. Nathaniel Kellum, surety, makes oath Susannah is of lawful age. Charles also makes oath he is of lawful age.

28 February 1784. Henry CONE and Mary Connelly. Sur. Benjamin Ward. Robert Williams, guardian of Mary, consents for her and states she is the orphan of James Connelly.

28 February 1785. Willis CONE and Sukey Connor. Sur. John Lambert.

5 January 1791. John CONNER and Mourning Hyllard. Sur. Wildridge Smith. William Byrd makes oath Mourning is of lawful age.

31 October 1753. Roderick CONNER and Margaret Scott. Sur. John Jones.

23 April 1763. John CONNOR and Elizabeth Jenings. Sur. Isaac Luke.

9 July 1785. Thomas CONNOR and Mrs. Margaret Conner. Sur. John Lambert.

17 June 1755. Joshua CONNYER and Jane Davis. Sur. Arthur Moseley.

11 August 1741. John COOKE and Mrs. Eliza Boush. Sur. Samuel Boush.

21 November 1782. Arthur COOPER and Mary Gordon. Sur. John Thomas.

3 July 1783. Arthur COOPER and Peggy McHenry. Sur. Thomas James.

15 January 1770. Charles COOPER and Mrs. Ann Dale. Sur. Chapman Manson.

21 March 1778. Charles COOPER and Mary Simmons. Sur. Arthur Cooper.

19 April 1787. Charles COOPER and Rosanna Ishon. Sur. James Oast.

21 June 1783. David COOPER and Nancy Dogget. Sur. Joshua Peed.

5 November 1764. Joel COOPER and Courtney Roberts. Sur. Lemuel Roberts.

1 October 1787. Solomon COOPER and Mary Walmsley. Sur. Thomas Walmsley. Married 2 October 1787 by Rev. Walker Maury.

— June 1790. Wilborn COOPER and Elizabeth Garnes. Married by Rev. Arthur Emmerson.

22 February 1782. William COOPER and Sally Wilder. Sur. Maximilian Marley.

6 December 1784. Thomas COPELAND and Charity Kinder. Sur. Robert Kinder.

23 April 1763. William COPELAND and Maren Porter. Sur. James Dickson.

17 November 1762. Gawin CORBIN and Joanna Tucker, dau. of Robert Tucker, who consents for her. Sur. Richard Holt.

26 March 1789. James CORDILL and Dorrity Stamers. Sur. Martin Doyle.

21 February 1772. Henry CORNICK and Mary Jeffery, orphan of Aaron Jeffery. Sur. Philip Carbery.

16 January 1773. William CORNICK and Mary Ashley. Sur. George Webb.

3 May 1756. John CORPREW and Euphan Wilson. Sur. William Nicholson.

7 April 1764. John CORPREW and Sarah Smith. Sur. Charles Smith.

8 April 1791. William CORRAN and Ann Willoughby. Sur. John Spellaman.

19 April 1768. William COSBY and Mary Pasteur, dau. of James Pasteur, of St. Brides Glebe, who consents for her. Sur. John Pasteur.

29 May 1792. Samuel COTTER and Tamer Cherry. Sur. James Ballance.

4 July 1770. Lemuel COVERLY and Mrs. Winea Dameron. Sur. Joel Jackson.

22 July 1783. Thomas COWIE and Susanna Higgins. William Crocker, surety, makes oath that Susanna is of lawful age.

21 December 1771. Ezekiel COX and Ann King. Sur. Hardress Waller.

15 November 1787. William CRAGAL and Mrs. Bathiah Hodges. Sur. James Wilkins.

13 July 1791. Joseph CRAWFORD and Sally Poole. Sur. Nathaniel Murphy. Mrs. Mary Watson makes oath Sally, orphan of Nicholas Poole, is of lawful age.

2 October 1766. Matthew CRAWFORD and Ann Turner. Sur. James Miller.

15 December 1784. Bartholomew CRAWLEY and Mrs. Eleanor Spooner. Sur. John Mushraw.

15 December 1784. William Robert CRAWLEY and Mary Slaughter. Sur. John Sclater.

15 April 1790. Stephen CREECH and Mary Thomson. Married by Rev. Arthur Emmerson.

21 May 1787. Charles CREEKMORE and Mary Ballance. Henry Ballance, surety, makes oath Mary is of lawful age and is surety. Married 3 August 1787 by Rev. Needler Robinson.

2 June 1787. Tucker CREEKMORE and Mary Hodges, dau. of Thomas Hodges. Sur. John Poyner. Joab Hinbery makes oath Mary is of lawful age. Married 2 June 1787 by Rev. Needler Robinson.

16 April 1789. Wright CREEKMORE and Mrs. Elisabeth McPherson. Sur. David Creekmur.

18 February 1792. Jonah CREEKMUR and Mrs. Mary West. Sur. Samuel McPherson. Eli Creekmur, brother of Jonah, makes oath he is of lawful age. Wit. James Grimes, Sr. and Jesse Hanbury.

16 May 1792. Matthew CREEKMUR and Betty Anne Holstead. Sur. Smith Holstead.

19 October 1787. Peter CREEKMUR and Abigail Ballance. Sur. Mordecai Ballance. Note: Written on Bond is "her father consenting."

19 September 1791. Warren CREEKMUR and Fanny Cooper. Sur. Solomon Creekmur. Note: It is stated at the top of the bond that Warren is the son of Solomon Creekmur.

16 June 1783. William CROCKER and Rachael McKay. Sur. Robert Hobbs.

22 May 1790. William CROCKER and Mrs. Courtney Moore. Sur. James Arlington. Married 2 July 1790 by Rev. Arthur Emmerson.

6 January 1792. William CROCKER and Agness Culpeper, orphan of Reuben Culpeper. Caleb Hughes, surety, makes oath Agness is of lawful age.

2 June 1787. Benjamin CROW and Sally Morris. Sur. John Morris.

17 April 1782. William CRUMER and Keziah Peeton. Sur. George Clark.

4 March 1790. John CUFFEE and Sally Shafer. Sur. Lemuel Cuffee. Note: "John Cuffee, a free man, made oath before me that Sally Shafer, orphan of John Shafer, is upwards of twenty-one years of age." Jas. Taylor.

2 July 1789. John CULLEN and Elizabeth Colley. Sur. James Davis. Solomon Lambert makes oath that Elizabeth is the daughter of James Colley.

23 June 1792. Joseph CULPEPER and Mrs. Frances Owens. Sur. John Taylor.

5 November 1789. Samuel CULPEPER and Peggy Culpeper. Robert Fort, surety, makes oath that Peggy is the dau. of Joseph Culpeper. Married 14 November 1789 by Rev. Arthur Emmerson.

6 October 1792. Thomas CULPEPER and Lydia Richardson. Sur. Jeremiah Richardson. Married 9 October by Rev. Arthur Emmerson.

11 April 1791. William CULPEPER and Mrs. Nancy Deans. Sur. John Culpeper. Married April 12 by Rev. Arthur Emmerson.

23 November 1780. Willis CULPEPPER and Elizabeth Ellis. Sur. Thomas Ellis.

7 February 1778. William CUNNINGHAM and Elizabeth Whiddon, dau. of John Whiddon. Sur. Ralph Pickett. Ref: The Lower Norfolk County Virginia Antiquary.

6 February 1789. John CURLING and Edey Smith. Joseph Curling, surety, makes oath that Edey is the dau. of Richard Smith and is of lawful age.

28 August 1727. John DALE and Mrs. Mary Cartwright. Sur. Solomon Wilson.

7 August 1764. William DALE and Dinah Edwards. Sur. Thomas Edwards.

8 April 1783. Joshua DALING and Elizabeth Smith. Sur. Robinson Smyth.

21 June 1764. Robert DALLAS and Mrs. Sarah Camack. Sur. Samuel Boush and Thomas Davis. Ref: The Lower Norfolk County Virginia Antiquary.

26 February 1791. Josiah DARNELL and Grace Wilson, who consents for self. Sur. Kedar Old. Willis Wilson makes oath that Grace is of lawful age.

24 September 1789. William DAULEY and Lovey Foreman. Sur. Jacob Foreman. William makes oath he is the orphan of Jonathan Dauley and is of lawful age.

15 December 1791. Bennet DAVIS and Elisabeth Gordon, orphan of James Gordon. John Redd, surety, makes oath Elisabeth is of lawful age.

14 September 1791. David DAVIS and Nancy Gray. Sur. Robert Reins. Married 16 September by Rev. Arthur Emmerson.

21 November 1785. Isaac DAVIS and Mary Footit, dau. of William Footit, who consents for her. Sur. Robert Butt.

11 April 1765. Joshua DAVIS and Sarah Mitchell. Sur. Joseph Mitchell.

3 June 1728. Richard DAVIS and Mrs. Grace Murrow. Sur. Solomon Wilson.

15 November 1764. Capt. Edward DAVISON and Martha Herbert, dau. of William Herbert, who consents for her. Sur. Caleb Herbert. Wit. Reuben Herbert.

22 September 1784. Abraham DAWES and Mrs. Rebecca Mathias. Sur. Samuel Hatton.

14 October 1762. William DAY and Ann Shore. Sur. George Shore. Ann is dau. of Ann Shore, who consents for her and states she is 22 years of age. Wit. Benjamin Watson and Thomas Hall.

19 December 1791. Thomas DEALE and Margaret Etheridge. Sur. William Plummer. Married 30 December by Rev. Arthur Emmerson.

14 April 1783. Nathan DEANS and Sarah Batchelor. Sur. Thomas Batchelor.

25 May 1778. William DEANS and Mrs. Edith Bailey. Sur. Thomas Bruce.

1 November 1778. Pitre DE BLAN and Mrs. ____? Keaton. Sur. Thomas Dupont.

7 June 1790. Thomas DELANEY and Mrs. Mary Palmer. Sur. Francis Thorogood. Note: Bond written Thorowgood; signature Thorogood.

8 February 1768. Charles DENBY and Ann Owins. Sur. James Thelaball.

24 September 1777. Charles DENBY and Mrs. Susanna Thelaball. Sur. James Thelaball.

17 May 1790. Edward DENBY and Ann Manning. Sur. Andrew Bryan. Edward makes oath he is of lawful age.

2 August 1787. Emperough DENBY and Mary Noyall. Samuel Marshall, surety, makes oath that Mary is orphan of Nicholas Noyall and is of lawful age. Wit. Cary Hansford.

5 September 1787. Emprough DENBY and Mary Niol. Sur. James Denby. Emprough Denby makes oath that Mary Niol is of lawful age. Probably same as Emperough Denby and Mary Noyall.

24 September 1789. James DENBY and Dinah Colley. Edward Colley, surety, makes oath Dinah is the orphan of Edward Colley and consents for his sister.

30 October 1778. Lamuel DENBY and Peggy Reed. Sur. John Reed.

22 March 1793. Malachi DENBY and Ann Tigner. James Reed, surety, makes oath that Ann, orphan of Major Tigner, is of lawful age.

29 November 1760. Nathaniel DENBY and Mrs. Elizabeth Langley. Sur. Mathias Denby. Edward Denby, consents for his son, Nathaniel. Wit. John Hansford and John Ince, Jr.

28 April 1759. Samuel DENBY and Monica Williams. Sur. Willis Williams. Wit. Matthias Denby.

11 December 1783. William DENBY and Susanna Redd. Sur. John Redd.

2 November 1779. Willis DENBY and Elisabeth Redd. Sur. John Redd.

6 June 1767. Nathan DENNY and Bridget Guy, dau. of James Guy. Sur. Francis Wishart. Wit. Simon Holstead and John Guy.

18 April 1789. James DICKINSON and Mrs. Mary Dudley. Sur. John Brent.

17 July 1783. Thomas DICKINSON and Ann Thompson. Sur. Thomas Crafts.

29 August 1772. James DISON and Elizabeth Bramble, dau. of Willis Bramble, who consents for her. Sur. Hardress Waller. Wit. Edward Mitchell and David Davis.

29 August 1760. Jonathan DISON and Sarah Talbot, dau. of William Talbot, who consents for her. Sur. John Woodsid(e). Wit. Richard Frazier and John Cheshire, Jr.

19 June 1756. Pavy DISON and Jane Gawthony. Sur. John Cann.

11 November 1728. Phillip DISON and Susanna Phillipps. Sur. Francis Dison.

2 February 1771. William DONALDSON and Eliza: Arnott, dau. of James Arnott of Portsmouth, Virginia. Sur. John Scott. Ref: The Lower Norfolk County Virginia Antiquary.

21 May 1791. George DORSET and Hannah Culpepper, orphan of John Culpepper. Sur. Stephen Makins. Hannah makes oath she is of lawful age. Married 26 May by Rev. Arthur Emmerson.

18 October 1791. Peter DOSHER and Peggy Portlock. Sur. Abram Brownley. Note: Bond written Dosier; signature Dosher.

17 July 1779. Peter DOUGE and Mrs. Molly Evington. Sur. James Doudge. Note: Bond written Douge; signature Douzer.

24 December 1789. John DOYLE and Susanna Logan. Sur. Herman Plitt.

23 October 1792. Lewis DRAYTON and Mrs. Mary Cooper. Sur. John Wakefield.

26 February 1785. John DRINAN and Mary Doyle. Sur. John Shields.

3 April 1789. Matthias DRURY and Mrs. Mary Sparrow. Sur. George Smyth.

10 March 1788. Peter DUBACK and Elizabeth Hatton. Married by Rev. Arthur Emmerson.

1 April 1784. Anthony DUNN and Susanna Denby, dau. of Arthur Denby, who consents for her. Sur. James Boushell. Wit. Mathew Smison.

4 December 1760. John DUNN and Sarah Weatheradge, dau. of Elizabeth Pierce, who consents for her. Sur. Richard Wallace.

5 August 1789. Stephen DUNTON and Grace Hunt Wilkins. Sur. John Wilkins.

-- October 1736. William DUTTON and Mary Edwards. Sur. John Wallice.

27 August 1754. Peter DYES and Margaret Lewelling. Sur. Thomas Owins.

20 April 1780. George DYSON and Sarah Hilton. Sur. George Dison.

4 January 1783. Manor DYSON and Ann Lewelling. Sur. Thomas Lambert.

20 January 1757. Willis DYSON and Mary Conner. Sur. William Colley.

4 January 1792. James EASTER and Druscilla Fisher. Sur. Thomas James.

21 December 1789. Cornelius EASTWOOD and Betsy Grimes. Sur. Samuel Westcott.

23 January 1789. Capt. Mathias EASTWOOD and Elizabeth Moody, dau. of Mary Wootton, who consents for her. Married 24 January 1789 by Rev. Arthur Emmerson.

30 July 1784. John ECCLES and Sarah Williams, dau. of Mrs. Mary Williams who consents for her. Sur. Lemuel Williams.

22 February 1728/9. John EDMUNDS and Sarah Russell. Sur. Peter Norly Ellegood.

8 May 1779. Cornelius EDWARDS and Eliza: Herbert. Sur. Thomas Herbert.

18 November 1766. John EDWARDS and Rebecca Whiddon. Sur. James Leitch.

19 February 1770. John EDWARDS and Joice Carter. Sur. Hardress Waller.

10 January 1790. Oney EDWARDS and Molly Hancocke. Married by Rev. Arthur Emmerson.

8 December 1761. Peter EDWARDS and Mary Portlock. Sur. Thomas Edwards and John Portlock.

17 November 1773. Thomas EDWARDS, Jr., and Elisabeth Southerland. Sur. Thomas Herbert.

24 January 1792. Thomas EDWARDS, Jr. and Frances Ann Nash, dau. of Thomas Nash, Sr., who consents for her. Sur. William Nash.

18 July 1785. Godfrid EFFLER and Mrs. Anne Stroud. Sur. Robert Anderson. Note: Bond written Effler, signature, Eftler.

31 July 1717. James EGERTON and Mirium Tatem, dau. of Elizabeth Tatem, who consents for her. Sur. James Cumming. Wit. Rand. Edgerton and Moses Kedwood. James Egerton is of the Province of Maryland.

13 June 1774. William EGGLESTON and Ellen Whittle Davis. Sur. Thomas Davis.

15 April 1775. Jonathan EILBECK and Mary Talbot. Ref: The Lower Norfolk County Virginia Antiquary.

13 August 1724. John ELLEGOOD and Abigail Mason. Sur. Solomon Wilson. Wit. Tabitha Wilson.

19 December 1761. Peter Norley ELLEGOOD and Mary Thelaball. Sur. James Ashley. Note: Written on Bond Peter Norley Ellegood, signature Peter Nolley Ellegood.

20 August 1785. Peter ELLIOTT and Peggy Young. Sur. Charles Conner. Note: Both Peter and Peggy are free negroes.

8 October 1790. Peter ELLIOTT and Tamer Burgess. Sur. George Wright Burges(s).

26 July 1764. Robert ELLIOTT and ---------- (torn). Sur. Henry Rothery.

17 December 1791. Robert ELLIOTT and Abigail Happer. Sur. John Hodges.

4 September 1789. Samuel ELLIS and Margaret Deal, orphan of Richard Deal. Sur. George Collins. Samuel makes oath that Margaret is of lawful age. Married 17 September 1789 by Rev. Arthur Emmerson.

24 August 1765. John ELLISON and Mary Drury. Sur. William Smith.

14 June 1760. John EMMERSON and Dinah Williams. Sur. Robert Moorie.

25 February 1758. James ESTER and Elizabeth Hiley. Sur. Edward Hiley. Note: Bond written Ester, signature Esther.

17 December 1792. Bassett ETHEREDGE and Lydia Portlock, dau. of Lemuel Portlock. Lemuel Butt, surety, makes oath Lydia is of lawful age.

26 October 1789. Charles ETHEREDGE and Elizabeth McCoy, dau. of Caleb McCoy, who consents for her. Sur. Malachi McCoy. Wit. James Woodside.

20 December 1792. Charles ETHEREDGE and Patty Miller, ward of Charles Odeon, who consents for her. Sur. Samuel Etheredge. Wit. Patty Odeon and Nancy Odeon.

12 March 1792. Hillary ETHEREDGE and Patience Freeman, orphan of Samuel Freeman. Willis Wingate, surety, makes oath Patience is of lawful age.

9 February 1784. Edward ETHERIDGE and Mary Etheridge, dau. of Argyle Etheridge, who consents for her and is surety.

30 May 1785. Enos ETHERIDGE and Mary Stokes. Sur. Jonathan Stokes.

5 June 1790. John ETHERIDGE and Mary Insell. Sur. John Insell.

22 November 1784. Henry ETHERIDGE and Ann Ellis. John Jones, surety, is guardian to Ann; no relationship stated.

24 December 1790. John EVANS and Sarah Short, who consents for self. Sur. Frederick Walond.

13 September 1787. Joseph EVANS and Courtney Shipwash, dau. of Ambrous Shipwash, who consents for her. Sur. William Bressie. Wit. John Evans. Married 13 September 1787 by Rev. Needler Robinson.

12 March 1785. Thomas EVANS and Dinah Wood, dau. of William and Dinah Wood, who consent for her. Surety not named.

23 April 1759. William EVENS and Mary Keaton. Sur. Joseph Hodges, Sr.

7 March 1789. Francis EWELL and Elizabeth Leitch. Sur. William Ward.

21 May 1789. Jesse EWELL and Elizabeth Williams. Sur. John Smallwood.

11 January 1772. John EWING and Mary Morris. Sur. John Morris.

18 August 1792. John EWING and Margaret Avery. Sur. Wilson Williams.

8 January 1760. Severn EYRE and Margaret Taylor. Sur. John Willoughby.

2 August 1791. Richard FAISTON and Lydia Bacon. Sur. Richard Bacon.

18 November 1778. William FALLOWDOWN and Sarah Peyton. Sur. John Pool.

31 January 1769. George FARRER and Judith Dickson. Sur. Edmund Dickinson.

14 February 1773. Thomas FARRER and Elizabeth Lovitt, dau. of Adam Lovitt, deceased. Sur. Edward Moseley.

21 January 1767. William FARRER and Mary Lovett, dau. of Adam Lovett, deceased, of Princess Anne Co. Sur. William Simpson. Charles Gasking, guardian of Mary, consents for her. Wit. John Thomas. William is of Norfolk Borough.

20 April 1790. Ebenezer FATHERRA and Sarah Miars. Married by Rev. Arthur Emmerson.

5 January 1780. Joshua FENTRESS and Mary Cooper. Sur. Thomas Hoffler.

11 April 1758. Lancaster FENTRESS and Mary Etheredge. Sur. William Etheredge.

24 November 1787. Lancaster FENTRIS and Mary Murden. Sur. Maxmillian Murden.

30 March 1792. John FEREBEE and Mrs. Susanna Jolliffe. Sur. John Smith. Note: Following name of John Smith at top of bond is "(of Hill)".

24 February 1791. Thomas FERBY and Margaret Tumblin, orphan of John Tumblin. William Tomblin, surety, makes oath that Margaret is of lawful age.

15 September 1789. George FERGUSON and Lydia Miller. John Bully, surety, makes oath Lydia, orphan of James Miller, is of lawful age.

4 February 1758. Nathaniel FIFE and Eliza' Richards. Sur. Francis Peart.

19 April 1746. Solomon FIFE and Mary Drury. Sur. John Drewry.

14 September 1789. William FISHER and Mrs. Sarah Peed. Sur. John Reed.

16 November 1789. Horatio FITZGERALD and Betsy Burgess. Sur. John Burgess.

7 January 1788. Morris FITZGERALD and Anne Vallentine. Married by Rev. Arthur Emmerson.

27 June 1764. Anthony FLEMING and Mary Portlock. Sur. Samuel Portlock.

25 February 1768. Gardner FLEMING and Christian Smith. Sur. James Parker.

20 August 1792. Alexander FLETT and Mrs. Ann Davis. Sur. John Rampingdolph (Randolph).

30 August 1782. Ivy FOREMAN and Christian Griffin. Sur. William Bruce. Married 3 September 1782 by Rev. Edward Mintz.

5 May 1791. Ivy FOREMAN and Diana Ward, orphan of Thomas Ward. John Moore, surety, makes oath Diana is of lawful age.

8 October 1789. Richard FOREMAN and Sarah Jones, dau. of Margaret Jones, who consents for her. Sur. Simon Butt.

23 April 1786. William FOREMAN and Lydia Foreman. Married by Rev. Edward Mintz.

8 January 1765. Robert FORSYTH and Anne Dolson, or Delson. Sur. John Dunn.

26 November 1785. Henry Collier FOSTER and Sarah Wilson. Sur. George Wilson.

3 September 1791. John FOSTER and Ann Gumbly, dau. of Isaac Gumbly, who consents for her. Sur. Benjamin Crow. Wit. Ann Gumbley, John Moore and Matthew Bingley.

8 February 1790. Joseph FOSTER and Frances Bailey. James Tart, surety, makes oath that Frances, orphan of John Bailey, is of lawful age. Married 11 February 1790 by Rev. Arthur Emmerson.

6 August 1774. Mich: FREADLY and Mrs. Director McLachlan. Sur. Jacob Williams.

2 January 1790. George FREEMAN and Mary Pullen. Married by Rev. Arthur Emmerson.

7 February 1749. William FREEMAN and Tabitha Wilson, dau. of Solomon Wilson, who consents for her. Surety not named.

27 September 1783. Henry FRIDLEY and Director Fridley. Sur. George Collins.

27 January 1783. John FLEET and Mary Willis. Sur. Charles Tomer.

22 June 1791. James FULFORD and Lydia Mansfield. Sur. Edmund Mansfield.

30 April 1791. Joseph FULLGHAM and Jenny Taylor, orphan of James Taylor. Sur. Josiah Cowper. Jenny makes oath she is of lawful age. Married 2 May by Rev. Arthur Emmerson who refers to Jenny as Mary Taylor.

6 July 1758. Samuel GALT and Sarah Jefferies. Sur. Alexander Bruce.

19 August 1791. Alexander GAMMON and Mary Taylor, dau. of John Taylor. Sur. Maxi Stewart. Richard Gammon consents for his son Alexander. Charles Hodges makes oath that Mary is of lawful age. Wit. Joel Gammon and Jacob Shipwash.

11 October 1757. Charles Roff GARDNER and Elizabeth Rothery, dau. of Henry Rothery, who consents for her. Sur. Daniel Rothery. Wit. Matthew Rothery and Richard Rothery.

7 February 1784. Thomas GARDNER and Anne Jacobs. Sur. Peter Ward. Anne makes oath she is of lawful age, and that both her parents are dead.

29 November 1784. Anthony GARRET and Mrs. Sarah Jones. Sur. Jack Laycock.

23 September 1772. John GARRICK and Eliza' Gray. Sur. James Haldane.

21 April 1779. James GASKINGS and Nancey Morris. Sur. John Morris.

6 March 1779. Job GASKINGS and Leah Lamount. Sur. Laban Goffigon.

23 July 1774. Nick GAUTEIR and Frances Robinson. Sur. Cornelius Calvert.

28 April 1769. William GEORGE and Ann Simpson. Sur. Cloudes P. Cary.

20 February 1784. James GIFFARD and Mary Darby, or Darley. Sur. John Archer.

4 November 1790. James GILCOT and Mrs. Elizabeth Carrol. Sur. Benjamin Bolton. Married 19 November 1790 by Rev. Arthur Emmerson, who records John Gilbert.

14 September 1765. John GILCHRIST and Frances Campbell, dau. of Archibald Campbell, who consents for her. Sur. James Campbell.

Probably 1784. John GILCHRIST - remainder of bond badly torn.

17 June 1784. William GILLIES and Ann Grigory. Sur. John Patterson.

3 December 1779. John GOINS and Mrs. Mary Hodges. Sur. Nathan Bagnall.

14 January 1792. Cornelius GODFREY and Sarah Butt, dau. of Caleb Butt, deceased. John Murden, Sr., surety, makes oath Sarah is of lawful age.

24 July 1784. George GODFREY and Mrs. Anne Jacobs. Sur. David Ballentine.

23 June 1756. Matthew GODFREY and Abigail Porter. Sur. William Porter. Wit. Thomas Hardie and Thomas Wilson.

24 February 1784. Colonel Matthew GODFREY and Abigail Thelaball. Sur. Robert Boush. Note: The following footnote is found in the Lower Norfolk County Virginia Antiquary: "Abigail Thelaball is the dau. of Thomas Thelaball by his wife Elizabeth Wilson, dau. of Major James Wilson, son of Colonel James Wilson. Elizabeth, at the time of her marriage to Thomas Thelaball, was the widow of Maximillian Boush the 2nd of Princess Anne County, Va."

26 April 1762. John GODFREY and Ruth Weldon. Sur. George Abyvon.

12 October 1758. Nathaniel GODFREY and Eliza' Wakefield. Sur. George Abyvon.

23 December 1784. Nathaniel GODFREY and Isabella Kelsick. Sur. James Godfrey.

9 June 1783. William GODMAN and Ollife Barnes. Sur. Frederick Barnes.

11 November 1773. Labon GOFFEGON and Mary Veale. Sur. John Phillips.

30 December 1779. Laban GOFFIGAN and Elizabeth Hansford, dau. of Edward Hansford, who consents for her. Sur. John Hurt.

27 September 1792. Ralph GOFFIGON and Rhoda Lush. Sur. John Branan, Jr. Married 27 September by Rev. Arthur Emmerson.

28 July 1773. George GOLL and Ann Skinner. Sur. Richard Bickardick.

4 August 1763. Edward GOOD and Ann Avery. Sur. Paul Kingston. Mary Avery makes oath that Ann, the dau. of James and Mary Avery, was born 4 March 1742. (Mary Avery not identified.)

15 July 1779. William GOODCHILD and Sarah Childers. Sur. John Williamson.

5 May 1764. Alexander GORDON and Sarah Alexander. Sur. David Chevis.

23 February 1773. Alexander GORDON and Elizabeth Hodges. Sur. George Gordon.

14 July 1759. Capt. George GORDON and Martha Moseley. Sur. William Chisholm.

26 April 1767. George GORDON and Mrs. Eliza' Bruce. Sur. Alexander Gordon.

17 May 1784. George GORDON and Elizabeth Skinner. Sur. Richard Bickardick.

6 January 1789. James GORDON and Margaret Etheridge, orphan of David Etheridge. Robert Williams makes oath Margaret is of lawful age and he is surety.

12 March 1792. William GORDON and Mrs. Laetitia Griffin. Sur. Bennet Davis.

22 April 1783. Oliver GORTON and Elizabeth Nicholas. Sur. Richard Jarvis.

19 May 1791. John GRAVES and Mrs. Hannah Stafford. Sur. James Dikinuns. Note: Bond written Dickinson, signature Dikinuns.

10 January 1791. Robert GRAVES and Mrs. Lucretia Pader. Sur. Macon Lug. Robert makes oath he is of lawful age. Married 10 January by Rev. Thomas Armistead who writes Pedes.

18 May 1785. William GRAVES and Mrs. Mary Pratt. Sur. Robert Anderson.

11 December 1766. Benjamin Dingley GRAY and Sarah Bayne. Sur. Stephen Tankard.

23 January 1775. Benjamin Dingley GRAY and Mrs. Mary Grimes. Sur. Stephen Tankard.

26 September 1791. Adam GRIER and Sally Peed. Sur. George Peed.

23 November 1785. James GRIMES and Lois Hodges. Sur. Solomon Hodges.

30 November 1792. Jesse GRIMES and Margaret Mayle. Sur. John Hall.

10 February 1780. John GRIMES and Sally Veale. Sur. Demse Veale.

24 February 1785. Joshua GRIMES and Fanny Hall, dau. of William Hall, Sr., who consents for her. Wit. George Thomas Hall and William Wilson. No surety.

16 March 1769. Maxey GRIMES and Margaret Dale. Sur. William Dale.

29 January 1780. Thomas GRIMES and Mary Miars. Sur. Joshua Miars.

10 March 1789. Jacob GRUBB and Mrs. Elizabeth Spencer. Sur. Adam Alexander Leyll.

20 May 1762. Richard GURLEY and Mary Hamilton. Sur. John Tucker.

21 February 1775. Alexander GUTHERY and Sophia Proby. Sur. Paul Proby.

28 May 1773. Bayley GUY and Lockey Talbot, dau. of William Talbot, who consents for her. Sur. John Boush. Wit. James McCoy and Mark Talbott.

12 May 1756. Benjamin GUY and Jacamine Pead. Sur. Lazarest Pead.

1 June 1785. Henry GUY and Elisabeth Lambert, dau. of John Lambert. Sur. John Lambert.

13 November 1757. John Sheales GWIN and Eliza' Lowrey. Sur. Jonathan Dison. Charles Smith makes oath that the following was copied from the Elizabeth River Parish Register: "Elizabeth, daughter of Robert and Eliza' Lowry his wife was born Novr. 9th A.D. 1733."

19 August 1734. William GWINN and Eliza' Sheals. Sur. Ebenezer Stevens.

27 February 1763. Daniel GWYN and Mrs. Mary Jones. Sur. Samuel Boush.

29 June 1779. Goldsbery HACKETT and Leah Andrews. Sur. Richard Jarvis.

31 December 1759. James HALL and Mary Robe. Sur. George Chamberlaine.

21 August 1775. John HALL and Mrs. Eliza' Phillips. Sur. Laban Goffigon.

25 March 1782. John HALL and Nancy McClean. Sur. James Leitch.

19 January 1789. John HALL and Polly Mushrow. Sur. John Mushroe. Married 19 January 1789 by Rev. Arthur Emmerson, who wrote Hale, not Hall.

7 May 1792. Joseph HALL and Elizabeth Bass. Sur. Joseph Bass.

30 April 1752. John HAMILTON and Patience Russell. Sur. George Chamberlaine.

5 January 1792. William HAMMOND and Lydia Colley, dau. of John Colley, deceased. Edward Colley, surety, makes oath Lydia is of lawful age. William makes oath he is also of lawful age.

15 January 1778. James HANBURY and Nancy Avary, dau. of Euphan Avary, who consents for her. Sur. Matthew Maund.

16 November 1792. John HANBURY and Sally Footit, orphan of William
Footit. Stephen Hodges, surety, makes oath Sally is of lawful age.

19 October 1792. William HANBURY and Agness Ballentine, dau. of Joseph
Ballentine, who consents for her. Sur. James Mills. Wit. William
Southerlin and John Bell.

1 April 1789. Willis HANBURY and Jemimah Stewart, dau. of John Stewart,
who consents for her. Sur. Caleb Hewlitt. Wit. Josiah Hanbury.
Married 2 April 1789 by Rev. Arthur Emmerson.

13 February 1778. Job HANBURY and Phebe Williams, dau. of Thomas
Williams. Ref: The Lower Norfolk County Virginia Antiquary.

29 March 1731/2. Simon HANCOCK, Jr., and Apphia Malbone. Surety not
named. Simon is of Princess Anne County, Va.

14 October 1787 or 1788. Josiah HANDBURY and Jemima Hewit. Married
by Rev. Arthur Emmerson.

28 December 1792. George HANEY and Mrs. Peggy Williams. Sur. George
Boush.

15 July 1784. Edward HANSFORD and Ann Kidd, dau. of John Kid, who
consents for her. Sur. James Gaskings. Wit. Laban Goffigon. Note:
Bond written Kidd, signature of father, Kid.

3 October 1753. Lewis HANSFORD and Ann Taylor. Sur. Samuel Boush, Jr.

20 April 1780. Leven HAOS and Mrs. Elisabeth Blake. Sur. Paul Oweins.

27 April 1760. Samuel HAPPER and Mary Porter. Sur. Matthew Godfrey.

25 July 1765. William HAPPER and Elizabeth (Betsy) Wilson, dau. of
Simon Wilson, who consents for her. Sur. Thomas Newton, Jr.

11 October 1759. William HAPPER and Frances Wilson. Sur. Josiah
Wilson. Josiah Smith, guardian of William, consents for him.

17 January 1736/7. Henry HARBERT and Abigail Cawson. Sur. Thomas
Harbart. Wit. Thomas Wright and Alexander McPherson.

2 January 1771. Joseph HARDING and Mary Herbert, dau. of Markam and
Mary Herbert. Mary Herbert consents for Mary and makes oath she is of
lawful age.

22 February 1787. Doctor Joseph HARDING and Mary Happer. George Kelly,
guardian of Mary, consents for her and is surety. Married 22 February
1787 by Rev. Walker Maury.

15 June 1787. John HARDMAN and Elisabeth Lamount. Sur. Ralph Pigot.

2 August 1760. John HARDY and Eliza' Walmsley. Sur. George Hensley.

11 March 1769. John HARDY and Elizabeth Wittingham. Sur. Robert Banks.

2 February 1790. John HARDY and Hannah Wilson. Sur. Thomas Owen. Married 7 February 1790 by Rev. Arthur Emmerson.

13 November 1792. Samuel HARE and Isabella Hodges. Sur. James Hodgis.

5 October 1792. George HARNAGE and Peggy Millow, dau. of William Millow, who consents for her. Sur. William Whitfield. Wit. John Nicolos and John Cox. Married 6 October by Rev. Arthur Emmerson. Note: Bond written Melow, consent written Millow.

27 December 1791. John HARNAGE and Olive Godman. Married by Rev. Arthur Emmerson.

16 August 1751. David HARPER and Mary Maning. Sur. John Maning.

14 December 1784. David HARPER and Mary Butt. Sur. Wilson Butt.

24 November 1791. James HARPER and Ann Dunn. Sur. Joseph Campbell.

5 January 1792. James HARPER and Anne Williams. Married by Rev. Arthur Emmerson.

24 March 1791. William HARPER and Dinah Grant. Absolom Grant, surety, makes oath that Dinah is of lawful age. William also makes oath he is of lawful age.

20 July 1771. John HARRIS and Mrs. Mary Scott. Sur. Francis Wishart.

22 January 1790. Samuel HARRIS and Nancy Carney. Married by Rev. Arthur Emmerson.

1 September 1789. Alexander Harvey and Margaret Langley. John Williams, surety, makes oath Margaret is orphan of Samuel Langley, deceased, and is of lawful age.

17 January 1775. William HARVEY and Frances Ker. Sur. Thomas Newton, Jr.

28 April 1791. John HARVY and Mrs. Molly Bashaw. Sur. John Burgess.

12 November 1766. Francis HATTON and Margaret Manning. Sur. Robert Bowers. Ann Manning makes oath her dau. Margaret, was born 18 August 1745.

23 June 1785. Samuel HATTON and Anne Mayle. Sur. William Goodchild. Geo. Thos. Hall consents for the marriage.

29 June 1779. Collen HAY and Betty Buckley. Sur. William Day.

6 July 1791. James HAYES and Mrs. Nancy Wilson. Sur. John Mot. Married 8 July by Rev. Arthur Emmerson.

27 December 1791. Lewis HAYDEN and Mrs. Elizabeth Browning. Sur. James McDorman. Married 28 December by Rev. Arthur Emmerson.

23 November 1785. Joshua HAYNES and Frances Hall, sister of George Thomas
Hall, who consents for her. Frances signs her own consent also. Sur.
Joshua Grimes.

23 December 1789. Joshua HAYNES and Ann Golt. Sur. George Golt. Married
23 December 1789 by Rev. Arthur Emmerson. Note: Rev. Emmerson writes
Ann Goll.

12 January 1784. Martin HEALY and Mrs. Mary Burgess. Sur. Alexander
Phillips. Note: Bond written Healy, signature Heely. Mary signs her
own consent.

4 September 1791. George HEATH and Phebe Manning. Wright Maning, surety,
makes oath his sister, Phebe, is of lawful age.

17 June 1773. John HEFFERMAN and Eliza' Horton. Sur. Samuel Kerr.

7 July 1785. James HENDERSON and Cherry Rutter. William M. Bruce, surety,
makes oath Cherry is orphan of John Rutter, deceased, and is of lawful age.

3 October 1789. Dowin HENDREN and Mary Rutter. Sur. John Owens. Downin
makes oath that Mary, orphan of John Rutter, is of lawful age.

25 May 1785. Ephraim HENDREN and Mrs. Margaret Duffie. Sur. Casper
Herreter.

20 January 1784. Argyle HERBERT and Mary Tucker. Sur. John Whiddon.

6 September 1768. Caleb HERBERT and Ann Nicholson. Sur. James Nicholson.

4 April 1785. Henry HERBERT and Polly Irish. Daniel Miars, surety, makes
oath Polly is of lawful age.

6 December 1785. Henry HERBERT and Peggy Portlock. Sur. Samuel Portlock.

28 May 1746. Hillary HERBERT and Elizabeth Veal. Sur. Thomas Veal.

18 January 1758. Hillary HERBERT and Jane Miles. Sur. Edward Miles.

2 March 1774. James HERBERT and Diana Tatem, dau. of Dinah Tatem, who
consents for her. Sur. Caleb Herbert. Wit. William Hunter.

6 September 1791. John HERBERT and Mrs. Mary Bartee. Sur. John Brown.

30 November 1792. Peter HERBERT and Peggy Sparrow, orphan of Peter Sparrow.
Reuben Herbert, surety, makes oath Peggy is of lawful age.

14 June 1765. Ruben HERBERT and Betty Sparrow. Sur. Peter Sparrow.

12 May 1767. Thomas HERBERT and Sophia Edwards. Sur. Thomas Edwards.

4 July 1778. Thomas HERBERT and Mrs. Ann Whiddon. Sur. Richard Herbert.

29 December 1742. William HERBERT and Janet Cawson. Sur. Markcom Herbert. The consent for Janet was given by John and Abigaill Whiddon (who was formerly the widow Cawson). Ref: The Lower Norfolk County Virginia Antiquary.

27 April 1779. William HERBERT and Mary Godfrey. Sur. Powell Reins.

22 January 1790. William Bartee HERBERT and Suckey Satchwell. Sur. Lemuel Williams.

27 January 1783. Joseph HEWIT and Ann Thenabal. Sur. Obadiah Mason.

20 October 1792. Caleb HEWLITT and Lydia Millison, dau. of Jacob Millison of New Mill Creek, who consents for her. Sur. Alexander Ferebee. Wit. John Millison and Robert Routh.

29 August 1754. Francis HEWLITT and Mary Hodges. Sur. John Hewlitt.

24 January 1791. George HIGGINS and Mrs. Rosanna Cooper. Sur. George Harvy.

11 December 1790. William HIGGINS and Judy Burns. Sur. James Carrol. Anna Brown makes oath that Judy is of lawful age.

28 December 1774. Charles HILL and Elizabeth Dale. Sur. John Reins.

1 May 1731. John HILL and Mrs. Margaret Wilson. Sur. Solomon Wilson. Wit. Edward Lewelling.

5 February 1785. James HILLIN and Tamer Lambert. Sur. Solomon Lambert.

24 August 1768. Nathaniel HILLTON and Susannah Bailey. Sur. Nicholas Poole.

22 September 1790. Charles HODGES and Peggy Savells, dau. of Daniel Savells, who consents for her. Sur. Roger Hodges. Wit. Josua Smith.

7 February 1778. Ferebee HODGES and Mary Frier. Sur. William Stroud.

7 August 1792. James HODGES and Mrs. Sarah Dison. Sur. John Talbot.

3 February 1790. Joel HODGES and Mary Wright. Sur. John Wright.

10 April 1760. Joseph HODGES, Jr., and Ann Balentine. Sur. Archibald Williamson.

1 October 1779. Joseph HODGES and Ann McCloud. Sur. William Stroud. Nathan Bagnall, guardian of Ann, consents for her.

10 March 1783. Joseph HODGES and Molly Etheridge. Sur. Enoch Etheredge.

21 February 1789. Joseph HODGES and Nancy Scott. Sur. Ezekiel Drummond. Joseph makes oath that Nancy is the orphan of George Scott, and is of lawful age.

21 September 1765. Josiah HODGES and Mary Ewell. Sur. John Williamson. Unice Morgan, sister of Mary, makes oath that she is of lawful age.

10 October 1789. Rowland HODGES and Mrs. Elizabeth Wilson. Sur. Ezekiel Drummond.

27 December 1790. William HODGES and Tamar Creekmur. Moses McPherson, surety, makes oath Tamar, the orphan of Markham Creekmur, is of lawful age.

11 May 1744. William HODGHON and Eliza' Mesler. Sur. Lodewyck Messler.

14 December 1791. James HODGIS and Catherine Moore, dau. of John Moore, who consents for her. Sur. William Whitfield. Wit. Stephen Sikes and Alexander Ferebee. Married 15 December by Rev. Arthur Emmerson. Note: Bond written Hodges, signature Hodgis.

29 June 1760. John HODGIS and Lydia Thomas. Sur. Thomas Creech.

9 September 1783. William HODGIS and Mrs. Charity Carney. Sur. John Moore.

22 February 1785. William HODGIS and Sarah Deans. Sur. William Deans. Note: Written in Bond after name of Sarah Deans are the words "With her father's consent".

27 April 1775. Francis HODGSON and Mrs. Mary Burton. Sur. William King.

31 August 1775. John HODGSON and Ann Newton, dau. of Rebecca Newton. Sur. Bassett Moseley. Ref: The Lower Norfolk County Virginia Antiquary.

3 June 1777. Thomas Hoffler and Sarah Cooper. Sur. Laban Goffigon.

1 June 1768. Josiah HOFFMIRE and Courtney Foreman, dau. of Alexander Foreman, who consents for her. Sur. Charles Smallwood.

26 May 1783. Nathaniel HOGGARD and Mary Gardner. Sur. William Wormington.

9 August 1791. Thomas HOLDNESS and Mary Hughes. Sur. Corbin Bracket. Thomas makes oath he and Mary are both of lawful age. Married 10 August by Rev. Arthur Emmerson.

10 February 1792. John HOLLETT and Mary Fredlee, orphan of Henry Fredlee. Wilson Williams, surety, makes oath that Mary is his ward. Married 11 February by Rev. Arthur Emmerson.

22 January 1778. John HOLLOWELL and Mrs. Mary Walker. Sur. George Oldner.

3 August 1784. John HOLLOWAY and Juley Grimes, dau. of Ann Grimes, who consents for her. Sur. William Grimes. Wit. George Phillips and Aaron Pullen.

15 February 1783. Joseph HOLMES and Ann Peede. Sur. John Brannan.

24 September 1791. Nicholas HOLMES and Ann Millison. Sur. William Millison. Note: Bond written Holmes, signature Homes.

17 June 1784. Robert HOLMES and Mary Wilson. Sur. Charles Wilson.

28 April 1791. Charles HOLSTEAD and Courtney Butt. Sur. Benjamin Butt.

7 May 1785. Mathias HOLSTEAD and Lydia Grimes, dau. of Charles Grimes, who consents for her. Sur. Simon Holstead.

31 December 1789. Mathias HOLSTEAD and Lydia Miller, dau. of Benjamin Miller, Jr., who consents for her. Sur. Jesse Jones. Wit. Joseph Hodges.

13 December 1728. Simon HOLSTEAD and Ann Mathias. Sur. William Portlock.

6 January 1768. Thomas HOLSTEAD and Mrs. Sarah Northcott. Sur. Giles Randolph.

29 September 1753. James HOLT and Ann Osheal. Sur. Samuel Boush, Sr. The following consent, addressed to Samuel Boush, Jr., is attached to the bond: "Child, I desire you'l issue marriage Lycense for Mr. James Holt with your sister Osheal" (et cetera). "Your Indulgt father, Sam'l Boush."

5 January 1792. John E. HOLT and Sarah Lee, orphan of John Lee. Sur. Samuel Livingston. Jane Lee, mother of Sarah, consents for her. Joseph Brown makes oath Sarah is of lawful age.

24 December 1790. Stephen HOPKINS and Mrs. Elizabeth Wrighting. Sur. James Simmons.

5 January 1792. Stephen HOPKINS and Ann Coverley. Sur. Archibald Parks. Ann makes oath she is of lawful age and states the Family Bible, in which her birth is recorded, was in the home of John Warren of Tanners Creek about a year ago.

31 July 1778. Walter HOPKINS and Abigail Herbert, dau. of Henry Herbert. Sur. Thomas Charlton. Ref: The Lower Norfolk County Virginia Antiquary.

16 March 1791. Caleb HUGHES and Sarah Culpeper. Thomas Culpeper, surety, of Western Branch, makes oath his sister, Sarah, is of lawful age.

11 July 1772. John HUGHES and Philarity Giles. Sur. Joseph Harding. Thomas Peirce, guardian of Philarity, makes oath she is of lawful age and of Norfolk County, and gives his consent. John Hughes is referred to as a Mariner. Wit. Arthur Smith and Sampson Wilson.

12 October 1790. Caleb HUMPHRIS and Kezia Sikes, dau. of Mary Sikes, who consents for her and makes oath she is of lawful age. Sur. William Ballentine.

15 February 1768. John HUNTER and Mrs. Mary Nicholson. Sur. Jonathan Dison.

4 January 1783. John HUNTER and Euphan Wilson, dau. of Col. Josiah Wilson, who consents for her. Sur. Jacob Hunter.

7 May 1759. John HURT and Mrs. Mary Ivy. Sur. Richard Brown.

24 November 1766. John HUTCHINGS, Jr., and Ann Ramsay. Sur. Samuel Boush.

4 December 1760. Joseph HUTCHINGS and Sarah Smith, dau. of Josiah Smith, who consents for her. Sur. George Abyvon.

21 February 1754. Stephen HUTCHINGS and Sarah Portlock. Sur. John Portlock.

22 September 1753. Zachariah HUTCHINS and Dinah Inkson. Sur. John Hamilton.

13 September 1754. John HUTTON and Flora Hiley. Sur. Edward Hiley.

26 September 1761. John HUTTON and Margaret Boyd. Sur. Mathias Denby. Mary Boyd, sister of Margaret, makes oath she was born 25 May 1738.

29 June 1774. Samuel INGLIS and Ann Aitchison, dau. of William Aitchison, who consents for her. Sur. James Parker.

7 October 1775. William INGRAM and Ann Talbutt. Sur. Robert Langley.

5 October 1790. Nicholas INSELL and Prudence Maund, orphan of Meriot Maund. Sur. John Cherry. Nicholas makes oath Prudence is of lawful age.

25 September 1785. John ISDELL and Anne Josey. Sur. Thomas Powell.

12 March 1785. James IVES and Lydia Lewelling. Sur. John Talbott and Spieavy Wyat. Note: Written in Bond is, "With their guardian's consent".

4 June 1746. Robert IVES and Cosiah Johnson. Sur. Charles Smith.

— November 1728. James IVY and Mary Furlong. Sur. Solomon Wilson. Note: Part of date torn.

4 June 1760. John IVY, Jr. and Elizabeth Nash. Sur. Matthew Miller. John is son of William Ivy, who consents for him.

18 March 1784. Samuel IVY and Ann Carney, dau. of William Carney. Sur. James Jolliff. Ann makes oath she was 24 years of age on 4th of October last. Married 21 March 1784 by Rev. Edward Mintz.

8 October 1754. Joel JACKSON and Frances Lowery. Sur. John Peyton.

6 October 1744. Richard JACKSON and Dinah Lewling. Sur. Abel Lewelling.

7 November 1723. Robert JACKSON and Eliza Brett. Sur. Solomon Wilson. Wit. John Brett and Paul Portlock.

29 April 1778. Thomas JACOBS and Ann Mather. Sur. Lemuel Godfrey.

15 October 1742. Henry JAMASON and Mary Stanley. Sur. James Oast.
Richard Stanley consents for Mary; no relationship given.

26 May 1784. Christopher JAMES and Elisabeth Denby. Sur. Samuel Denby.

26 December 1785. Christopher JAMES and Mary Josey. Sur. Thomas James.

7 March 1789. Christopher JAMES and Martha Smithson. Sur. John Nichols.
Matthew Godfrey makes oath Martha is of lawful age.

7 October 1790. John JAMES and Mary Lowrey. Sur. Thomas James. Thomas
Lowry, father of Mary, consents for her and states she was of lawful age
on 13 January 1789. Wit. George Barrett and James Easter.

-- June 1783. Thomas JAMES and Elizabeth Jocey. Sur. Arthur Cooper.
Note: Date in June omitted from Bond.

8 September 1761. Neil JAMIESON and Fernelia Ellegood. Sur. Samuel
Boush.

23 April 1774. William JAQUES and Mrs. Ann Watson. Sur. James Walker.

6 July 1790. Joseph JARRET and Hannah Webb. William Newbold, surety,
makes oath Hannah is of lawful age.

21 January 1792. Edward JARVIS and Mrs. Mason Pritchard. Sur. John Jarvis.
Note: See Tubman Laws.

28 May 1792. Elijah JARVIS and Susanna Silverthorn. Edmond Warriner,
surety, makes oath Susanna is of lawful age.

30 May 1770. Robert JARVIS and Sarah Manning. Sur. John Manning and
Seth Portlock.

10 April 1787. David JEFFERSON and Mrs. Anne Kelsick. Sur. J. G. Martin.

5 February 1777. Aaron Jeffery and Sarah Silvester. Sur. Benjamin Weston.

27 April 1775. Robert JERVIS and Keziah Portlock. Sur. Lemuel Portlock.

10 September 1787. William JINKINS and Ellender Walmsley. Sur. Thomas
Walmsley. Married 11 September 1787 by Rev. Walker Maury.

16 November 1792. James JILCOT and Mrs. Mary Conner. Sur. Thomas Wilson.

19 March 1763. John JOHNSON and Frances Lewelling. Sur. Samuel Langley.

1 August 1787. Thomas JOHNSON and Isabella Kirkley. Married by Rev.
Walker Maury.

5 May 1789. James JOLLIFF and Martha Furbee. Sur. Charles Ferebee.

24 October 1789. William JOLLIFF and Susannah Boushell. Sur. John Smith. William makes oath that Susannah, orphan of Thomas Boushell, is of lawful age.

18 October 1784. John JONES and Mary Murden. John Murden, Jr., surety, makes oath that Mary, dau. of Jermiah Murden, deceased, is of lawful age.

10 February 1792. John JONES and Mrs. Mary Etheridge. Sur. David Fentress.

17 July 1790. Loftis JONES and Elizabeth Smith. Lewis Marshall, surety, makes oath that Elizabeth, orphan of Thomas Smith, is of lawful age.

3 October 1722. Nehemiah JONES and Edith Butt. Sur. Robert Butt. Wit. Solomon Butt, Lemuel Thelaball and Adam Thorogood.

22 February 1790. Richard JONES and Ann Synott, who consents for self. Sur. Alexander Peter.

7 January 1780. Samuel JONES and Martha Godfrey, dau. of James Godfrey. Sur. Nathaniel Godfrey.

2 August 1792. Samuel JONES and Ann Ferbee. John Waddell, surety, makes oath Ann, an orphan, is of lawful age.

29 July 1784. Samuel JONES and Mary Pippin. Sur. Goldsbery Hackett.

22 May 1760. William JONES and Mary Pedes. Sur. Richard Obrien.

16 June 1785. William JONES and Margaret Ward. Sur. Caleb Ward. Wit. Margaret Ward.

24 February 1792. Francis JORDAN and Sarah Boyles. Sur. James Boyles.

24 February 1787. John JORDAN and Margaret Frost. Married by Rev. Walker Maury.

9 May 1789. Jonathan KAY and Mrs. Louisa Grimes. Sur. John Harnage. Married 16 May 1789 by Rev. Arthur Emmerson.

22 July 1758. William KAY and Elizabeth Dale. Sur. Daniel Dale. Note: Bond written Kay, signature Kays.

10 February 1785. John KEARNES and Margaret Elliott, dau. of Robert Elliot, who consents for her. Sur. Thomas Mathews. Note: Difference in spelling of Elliot(t).

5 March 1770. Absalom KEEBLE and Mildred Gwynn. Sur. Walter Gwyn. Note: Difference in spelling of Gwyn(n).

19 February 1771. Robert KEEBLE and Dorothy Reade. Sur. James Reade.

6 October 1792. Alexander KEELING and Elizabeth Blake, dau. of Mrs. Elizabeth Howse, who consents for her. Sur. Thomas Roberts. Christopher ————. guardian of Alexander, consents for him. Wit. John Gisbon. Note: Mrs. Elizabeth Blake (Howse) was appointed guardian for her dau. Elizabeth, April 1786.

30 August 1791. Henry KEELING and Katy Hennicke. Frederick Hennicke, surety, makes oath his sister, Katy, is of lawful age.

29 September 1792. Henry KEELING and Anne Wilder. Sur. William Whitfield.

3 April 1790. Thomas KEELING and Mary Grimes. Sur. George Collins. Thomas makes oath he is of lawful age. Married 4 April 1790 by Rev. Arthur Emmerson.

17 May 1777. Thorowgood KEELING and Mrs. Mary Bridger. Sur. Nathaniel Burgess.

13 March 1777. Alexander KEITH and Mary Denby. Sur. Richard Lishman.

13 May 1791. Peter KELLUM and Adah Robins. Sur. William Jones.

2 July 1783. George KELLY and Katy Godfrey. Sur. Alexander Moseley.

19 May 1769. Richard KELSICK and Ann Porter. Sur. Matthew Godfrey.

22 January 1790. Richard KELSICK and Dolly Pritchard. Sur. Richard Barr.

4 October 1759. Capt. John KELSO and Margaret Williamson. Sur. John Williamson.

6 July 1787. John KENNEDY and Polly Wilson. Sur. Thomas West. Married 7 July 1787 by Rev. Needler Robinson. Note: "Sir, Please Grant Mr. Jno. Kennedy License to be married to Polly Wilson he having obtained my father's consent. I am sir, Yr. Humble Svt. Willis Wilson, Jr."

18 November 1785. Andrew KIDD and Elizabeth Murray. Sur. Edward Hansford.

12 December 1754. William KIDD and Hannah Duche. Sur. Andrew Duche.

31 October 1784. Peter KILGREW and Elisabeth Simmons. Sur. Solomon Lambert. Elisabeth makes oath she is of lawful age.

12 March 1762. Alexander KINCAID and Martha Brodie. Sur. Robert Waller.

19 April 1792. Robert KINDER, Jr. and Martha Godfrey. Sur. James Hodges, Jr. Martha makes oath she is the daughter of Matthew Godfrey and Mary and that she is 21 years old this day.

21 December 1789. Francis KING and Mrs. Elizabeth Furnace. Sur. Adam Alexander Leyll.

12 May 1791. Miles KING and Sarah Lockhart, orphan of James Lockhart. Sur. Barnaby Carney. Miles makes oath Sarah is of lawful age.

9 April 1792. Jacob KISNER and Nanny Beetley. Sur. Francis Beetley.

26 November 1762. Thomas KNIGHT and Ann ------ing. Sur. Cornelius Calvert. Note: This Bond is mouse eaten and a part of Ann's name is missing.

20 December 1792. James LAMBERT and Mary Wilson. Sur. William Millison.

20 December 1792. Thomas LAMBERT and Agness Wilkins, dau. of John Wilkins, Sr., who consents for her. Sur. John Wilkins. Wit. John Wilkins, Jr. and John Holland.

2 June 1787. Solomon LAMBERT and Mary Jackson. Sur. John Jackson. Married 3 September 1787 by Rev. Walker Maury.

19 September 1765. Henry LAMOUNT and Susannah Milburn. Sur. Richard Bickardick. Note: Bond written Lamount, signature Lemon.

11 March 1791. Jesse LAND and Kezia Ball, dau. of Willis Ball. Sur. John Woodland. Jesse makes oath Kezia is of lawful age.

3 December 1763. William Sealy LANE and Courtney Prata. Sur. Nathaniel Fife.

20 December 1783. Thomas LANDON and Mrs. Ann Peaton. Sur. Joshua Peyton.

28 July 1752. Absolam LANGLEY and Elizabeth Sceady. Sur. James Langley.

24 May 1731. James LANGLEY and Sarah Nickhalson. Sur. not named.

1 October 1771. James LANGLEY and Eliza' Snale. Christopher Snale of Princess Anne County, brother of Eliza', consents for her and is surety.

26 September 1792. John LANGLEY and Sally Harmon, dau. of George Harmon, who consents for her. Sur. John Wilkins. Wit. Jonathan Langley.

3 October 1765. Joseph LANGLEY and Elizabeth Ashley. Sur. John Ashley.

23 April 1772. Joseph LANGLEY and Sarah Butt. Sur. Edward Park.

26 April 1768. Lemuel LANGLEY and Sarah Butt. Sur. Josiah Wilson.

19 October 1760. Samuel LANGLEY and Elizabeth Lewelling. Sur. Zachariah Hutchings.

1 September 1779. William LANGLEY and Peggy Bartee. Sur. Samuel Portlock.

9 November 1779. Willis LANGLEY and Susanna Bruce. Sur. James Webb, Jr. Susanna makes oath that she is of lawful age.

11 March 1773. Thomas LANGSTON and Clotilda Sawyer Jones. Sur. John Jones. Ref: The Lower Norfolk County Virginia Antiquary.

18 November 1769. Thomas LARCHIN and Mrs. Eliza' Holt, dau. of Mary Holt. Sur. James Leitch. Wit. Thos. Veale.

3 August 1785. Daniel LASITER and Elizabeth Creech. Sur. James Tartt. Married 6 August 1785, by Rev. Edward Mintz.

6 December 1762. George LATHBURY and --------cca (Rebecca?) Baker. Sur. Samuel Farmar. Note: Part of Bond is mouse eaten.

15 May 1783. William LATTIMER and Mary Hodges, dau. of William Hodgis, who consents for her and is surety. William is of Nansemond County.

26 November 1791. Bartholomew LAWRENCE and Elizabeth Butt, dau. of Epaphroditus Butt. John Brooks, surety, makes oath Elizabeth is of lawful age. Married 15 December by Rev. Arthur Emmerson.

22 December 1783. Augustus LAWRENS and Elizabeth Miller. Sur. Arthur Cooper. Note: Bond written Lawrens, signature Laurentz.

21 January 1792. Tubman LAWS and Mrs. Mason Pritchard. Sur. Wilson Williams. Note: See Edward Jarvis.

29 June 1758. Anthony LAWSON and Mary Calvert. Sur. Maxmilian Calvert.

3 December 1792. John LEAK and Mrs. Anne Nosay, widow of Thomas Nosay. Sur. Joseph Cooper.

23 July 1785. William LEATHERBURY and Anne Stroud, whose guardian (not named) consents for her. Sur. Joshua Pead.

15 December 1785. John LEE and Frances Airs. Sur. William Jones.

4 December 1769. John LEE and Jane Brazill. Sur. John Livingston.

4 May 1784. Thomas LEE and Mary Ann McCoy, dau. of Richard McCoy, deceased. Sur. Thomas Thomas. Richard McCoy consents for his ward, Mary Ann. Wit. John McCoy and Willis McCoy.

13 November 1763. Daniel LEECH and Ann Rogers. Sur. Henry Wells.

29 November 1766. James LEITCH and Susanna Terry, dau. of Joanna Terry, who consents for her and who states she was born 12 September 1745. Sur. Robert Burn.

1 September 1774. James LEITCH and Sarah Yewill, dau. of Diana Yewill, who consents for her. Sur. William Ewell.

20 April 1778. John LELLO and Mary Wonycott. Sur. Edward Wonycott.

20 June 1775. John LELLS and Eliza' Larchen. Sur. George Bowness.

30 November 1774. George LESLIE and Mrs. Mary Williams. Sur. George Collins.

13 October 1792. Isaac LEVI and Judah Hill, orphan of William Hill. George Miller, surety, makes oath Judah is of lawful age.

31 October 1774. James LEWIS and Jane Wall. Sur. Jonathan Eilbeck.

18 October 1751. John LEWIS and Rachel Bingham. Sur. Patrick Kelly. Wit. John Willoughby.

16 February 1771. Peter LEWIS and Margaret Eyre. Sur. William Smith.

29 May 1771. William LEWIS and Sarah Taylor. Sur. Richard Taylor.

25 January 1790. Adam Alexander LEYLL and Mrs. Jenet Shields. Sur. David Leitch.

25 September 1729. James LIBBY and Sarah Wright. Sur. Thomas Martin.

1 February 1787. John LIGHTFOOT and Anne Wright. Sur. James Ramsey. Married 4 February 1787 by Rev. Walker Maury.

20 May 1761. John LINDSAY and Jane Drummond. Sur. Robert Moorie.

15 May 1784. Thomas LING and Mrs. Jenny Isorns. Sur. Samuel Blews.

21 September 1771. Richard LISHMAN and Agnes Thompson, dau. of Isaac Thompson. Sur. William Liddle.

4 February 1769. John LIVINGSTON and Ann Dunn. Sur. Benjamin Newbould.

7 December 1792. John LIVINGSTON and Tabitha Herbert. Sur. Caleb Herbert.

14 February 1787. Samuel LIVINGSTON and Margaret Herbert. Sur. Thomas Herbert. Married by Rev. Walker Maury.

26 December 1785. Samuel LOCKHART and Mary Watts, dau. of Dempsey Watts, who consents for her. Sur. Wright Maning. Wit. John Bacon.

17 May 1761. George LOGAN and Isabella Campbell. Sur. Archibald Campbell. Wit. Richard Price Kerby.

17 February 1749. John LLOYD and Eliza' Hall. Surety not named.

26 May 1771. Alexander LOVE and Elizabeth Calvert, dau. of Cornelius Calvert. Sur. James Gilchrist. Ref: The Lower Norfolk County Virginia Antiquary.

17 April 1789. Joseph LOVELAND and Peggy Griggs. Sur. John Britton. Married 18 April 1789 by Rev. Arthur Emmerson.

10 April 1789. James LOWE and Elizabeth Carter. Sur. Henry Lowe. Both Benjamin and Elizabeth Carter consent for their daughter, Elizabeth. Married 11 April 1789 by Rev. Arthur Emmerson.

23 December 1773. Thomas LOWREY and Sarah Wildair. Sur. William Ward.

28 July 1764. Jacob LOWRY and Judith Hilman. Sur. William Bowins.

21 August 1782. Isaac LUKE and Sarah Carbery. Sur. George Dyson.

24 March 1789. Paul D. LUKE and Mrs. Sarah Grimes. Sur. Edward Hansford.

11 May 1771. William LUKE and Sarah Murray. Sur. David Murray.

2 April 1763. Andrew LUSH and Mrs. Sarah Cooper. Sur. Francis Miller.

9 March 1789. John LYMBURN and Nancy Pearson, dau. of Mrs. Mary Pearson of Williamsburg, who consents for her. Sur. Matthew Pearson. Note: Nancy formerly of York County. Married 20 March 1789 by Rev. Arthur Emmerson.

18 October 1779. Richard MACCOY and Elisabeth Etheridge. Sur. Willis MacCoy.

11 November 1783. Richard MACCOY and Mrs. Ann Herbert. Sur. Seth Hebdon.

29 August 1772. William MACKIE and Eliza' Dale, or Doe. Sur. John Vallanier.

7 April 1737. Edward MAGEE and Mrs. Ann Wise. Sur. John Keen.

15 September 1783. Bernard MAGNIEN and Mrs. Margaret Rives. Name of surety illegible.

19 May 1723. Rehodolphus MALBONE and Mary Richardson. Sur. Peter Malbone. Wit. Solomon Wilson and John Fergison. "Mary is a Resident of Norfolk Town."

17 July 1783. Anthony MALO and Ann Denbigh. Sur. Joshua Ventris.

30 January 1785. Mitchell MANE and Mrs. Frances Doudge. Sur. Charles Rudder.

12 November 1762. Moses MANING and Lydia Smith. Sur. John Smith.

25 November 1790. James MANNING and Eda Perkins. Married by Rev. Arthur Emmerson.

24 December 1791. James MANNING and Faith Stewart, dau. of James Stewart, deceased. Sur. Joseph Roach. James makes oath he is of lawful age. Willis Sikes makes oath Faith is of lawful age.

7 September 1767. Reube MANNING and Dinah McCoy. Sur. Richard McCoy.

20 March 1775. William MARLEY and Anne Godfrey. Sur. James Godfrey.

24 May 1792. William MARLEY and Mrs. Priscilla Rogers. Sur. William Goodchild.

28 December 1764. Guivinies MARNES and Anna Maria Barocherfour, who consents for herself. Sur. Casper Herriter. Anna Maria makes oath that she was born in Reedingtown, Bucks County, Penna. in 1741.

3 September 1757. Capt. John MARNEX and Jemima Garroway. Sur. Charles Thomas.

11 February 1789. James MARNO and Disey Hodges. Sur. James Hodgis. Married 26 February 1789 by Rev. Arthur Emmerson.

21 November 1768. James MARSDON and Polly Calvert. Sur. Maximilian Calvert.

28 May 1792. Samuel MARSHALL and Patty Wyatt, orphan of Shadrack Wyatt. Nathan Miars, surety, makes oath Patty is of lawful age.

22 May 1784. Andrew MARTIN and Margaret Mohun. Sur. Richard Taylor. Robert Taylor, guardian of Margaret, gives consent for her.

9 March 1792. James MARTIN and Mrs. Mary Deal. Sur. Theophilus Cherry and Maxey Cherry.

21 July 1772. John MASON and Elizabeth Coverly. Sur. Dickerson Pryor.

17 August 1785. John MASON and Mrs. Elizabeth Denby. Sur. James Davis.

1 June 1758. Nathaniel Newton MASON and Ann Snale. Sur. John Hutchings.

20 November 1772. Robert MATHER and Ann Ballentine. Sur. Samuel Ballentine.

9 July 1773. Thomas MATHEWS and Mary Miller. Sur. John Hutchings.

15 September 1785. John MATHIAS and Hannah Barrington. Sur. James Statham.

22 July 1785. James MATTHEWS and Mrs. Ann Porter. Sur. Joshua Grimes.

22 May 1767. John MATTHIAS and Mary Barringer. Sur. Samuel Barrington.

9 August 1792. John MATTHIAS and Polly Williamson. Sur. John Singleton.

28 July 1792. Joshua MATTHIAS and Frances Wilson, ward of John Portlock, who consents for her. Sur. John Matthias. Wit. John Quarles.

20 March 1753. Lott MAUND and Mary Wright. Sur. George Felton.

25 September 1765. Mathew MAUND and Elizabeth Williams, dau. of John Williams, who consents for her. Sur. Thomas Bressie. Wit. Caleb Williams and Matthew Portlock.

23 August 1754. Charles MAYLE and Dinah Besan (or Bevan). Sur. George Poole.

28 March 1765. Doctor Charles MAYLE and Lydia Nash, dau. of Thomas Nash, Sr., who consents for her. Sur. Thomas Nash, Jr.

6 April 1767. James MAXWELL and Hellen Calvert. Sur. Samuel Boush.

6 April 1785. Thomas MAXWELL and Mrs. Sarah Jarvis. Sur. Joseph Warden.

20 February 1790. Thomas MAXWELL and Mrs. Susanna Holland. Sur. James Gardner.

29 October 1785. Duncan McBRIDE and Mrs. Sarah Sanford. Sur. James McBride.

11 February 1764. William McCAA and Sarah Brough. Sur. Richard Scott.

13 April 1769. John McCARIEL and Frances Freeman, dau. of William Freeman, who consents for her. Sur. William McCaa. Wit. George Kelly.

4 August 1763. John McCARTHIE and Mary Avery, dau. of James and Mary Avery. Sur. John Wills. Mary Avery makes oath that her dau. Mary was born 11 August 1740. Wit. John Lello, John Lello, Jr. and Richard Butt. Note: Bond written McCarthie, signature McCarthy.

8 January 1768. John MACLEAN and Suckie Talbot, dau. of Thomas Talbot, who consents for her. Sur. Goodrich Boush. Wit. Obiah Mason and Esther Godfrey.

27 January 1782. James McCLOUD and Frances Case. Sur. Henry Snail.

3 July 1792. Charles McCOY and Elizabeth Portlock, dau. of Lemuel Portlock, who consents for her. Sur. Kadar Dobbs.

18 March 1784. Joshua McCOY and Mrs. Sarah Etheridge. Sur. Henry Butt.

24 August 1784. William McCOY and Fanny Wiles, sister of Kezia MacCoy, who consents for her. Sur. Joshua McCoy.

7 February 1774. Robert McCULLY and Jane Sisson, dau. of William Sisson, who consents for her. Sur. Pate Dwyer. Wit. William Walker.

24 February 1792. Michael McDARMOTT and Ann Bryan. Sur. Eyre Blake. Michael makes oath that both he and Ann are of lawful age.

28 October 1789. Thomas McDORMAND and Mrs. Susannah Jasper. Sur. James McDormand. Colin C. Wills, brother of Susannah, makes oath she is of lawful age. Married 28 October 1789 by Rev. Arthur Emmerson.

22 July 1789. Archibald McDOUGAL and Martha Willoughby. Sur. Henry Bragg. Cornelius Calvert, Sr. makes oath Martha is of lawful age.

15 May 1784. James McDOWELL and Prudence Jarvis. Sur. Richard Jarvis. Note: Bond written McDowell, signature McDuell.

9 November 1731. Phillip McDOWELL and Sarah Drewry. Sur. John Drewry. Wit. John Smith and John Fife.

28 August 1790. Dugal McDUGAL and Mary Waterman. John Waterman, surety, consents for his sister Mary, and makes oath she is the orphan of Solomon Waterman, deceased, and is of lawful age. Note: Written Dugal McDugal in Bond, signature Dougal McDougal.

7 April 1784. Dannil McDURMUIR and Mrs. Ann Bayne. Sur. John Britton.

16 May 1785. James McENDLESS and Mary Ellison. Sur. John Shields.

11 February 1785. Alexander McFARLANE and Mary Playstead, dau. of Letitia Playstead, who consents for her. Surety not named.

1 September 1787. Archibald McGOUN and Mrs. Ann Hughes. Sur. Thomas Drury. Married 2 September 1787 by Rev. Walker Maury.

9 August 1784. William McKENNY and Mrs. Sarah Garnes. Sur. Matthias Moore.

24 December 1784. John McKENZIE and Hester Jenning. Sur. Jerry Connolly.

17 February 1785. Robert McLARTY and Mrs. Mary McClenahan. Sur. Matthew Douglass.

12 June 1762. Florence McMAMARA and Sarah Brodie. Sur. Philip Carbery. Note: The name Florence appears both in the Bond and the signature.

22 July 1732. Gilbert McNARY and Mary Wilson. Sur. Samuel Sweeny.

9 February 1742/3. Duncan McNEIL and Sarah Sparrow. Sur. William Portlock.

2 February 1791. John McPHERSON and Cloe Creekmur, orphan of Edward Creekmur. Tucker Creekmur, surety, makes oath Cloe is of lawful age.

18 January 1787. Moses McPHERSON and Mrs. Mary Etheridge. Sur. Charles Creekmur.

1 December 1773. Matthew McVIE and Susannah Darby. Sur. Joseph Pope.

8 June 1779. Joseph MEAD and Mary Pool. Sur. Robert McCully.

29 March 1764. Samuel MEADE and Elizabeth McCurdy. Sur. William Bowin. Esther Jackson, wife of John Jackson, makes oath that neither of Elizabeth's parents are living and that she is of lawful age. Wit. Samuel Boush.

27 December 1790. Bartholomew MEARS and Sarah Cooper. Sur. Jonathan Cooper.

4 January 1790. John MEDDAN and Mrs. Elizabeth Tumer. Sur. John Fulchiron.

11 April 1790. Robert MERCY and Sally Graham. Married by Rev. Arthur Emmerson.

2 April 1765. Jonathan MEREDITH and Eliza' Hodgson. Sur. Christopher Thistlewaite.

27 February 1790. Robert MERRITT and Polly Latham. George Oast, surety, makes oath that Polly is of lawful age.

15 December 1785. David MIARS and Sarah Ellis. Sur. Samuel Ellis.

8 January 1789. John MIARS and Mary Cherry. Sur. John Cherry. Married 9 February 1789 by Rev. Walker Maury.

17 June 1779. Joshua MIARS and Elisabeth Deans. Sur. William Bailey.

24 September 1744. Patrick MICALROY and Mary Pilkington. Sur. Davis Neal. Both Mary Pilkington and James Giles sign a consent for Patrick and Mary; no relationship stated.

19 October 1765. Joseph MIDDLETON and Elizabeth Ballentine. Sur. John Lewelling.

5 March 1782. John MIERS and Ann Hollowell, dau. of John Hollowell, who consents for her. Sur. George Wainwright.

20 August 1778. Aaron MILHADO and Mary Moore. Sur. Richard Brown.

1 December 1769. Benjamin MILLER and Frances Odean. Sur. Charles Odean. John Portlock consents for Frances; no relationship or guardianship stated. Wit. Enoch Etheredge and Lemuel Barrington.

16 October 1788. Caleb MILLER and Ann Philips. Married by Rev. Arthur Emmerson.

18 January 1787. Edward MILLER and Barbara Mansfield. Sur. Robert Mansfield.

24 March 1785. Hance MILLER and Dorcas Willis. Sur. Walter Willis.

29 March 1732/3. Henry MILLER and Elizabeth Godfrey. Surety not named.

8 August 1766. James MILLER and Elizabeth Avery. Sur. Edward Good. Mary Avery, mother of Elizabeth, makes oath she was born 5 December 1744. Wit. Richard Butt, Ann Good and Elizabeth Avery.

17 August 1791. Joel MILLER and Polly White, orphan of Gideon White. Sur. Kedar Old and Thomas Old. Polly makes oath she is of lawful age. Thomas Old is guardian of Joel Miller.

11 January 1791. Josiah MILLER and Nancy Phillips. Sur. Thomas Woodard.

31 January 1742. Matthias MILLER and Alif Ivy. Sur. Samuel Boush.

10 August 1787. William MILLER and Fornelia Williamson. Sur. John Williamson. Married 12 August 1787 by Rev. Needler Robinson.

22 February 1759. John MILLINER and Jane Robinson. Sur. Goodrich Boush. Consent: "Febry 22: 1759 - John Milenr Has my Consent to Mary ian Robson my Sarvint Woman. Given under my hand, Ashbury Sutton."

2 December 1785. James MILLOW and Mary Giles. Sur. James Boushell.

18 May 1782. William MILLOW and Mary Sharp. Sur. Jacob Williams.

23 August 1792. John MOHANES and Elizabeth Marley. Sur. William Morley.

31 July 1764. Joel MOHUN and Eliza' Nelson. Sur. Robert Elliot. Note: Bond written Mohun, signature Moon.

1 July 1790. Michet MONERY and Elizabeth Rudder. William Ballentine makes oath Mitchel Morning is of lawful age.

21 August 1758. William MOORE and Betsy Bird. Sur. James Bird.

20 May 1790. William MOORE and Elizabeth Brian. Sur. Robert Thompson.

12 June 1765. John MONTGOMERIE and Sarah Dyer Thelaball. Sur. James Thelaball.

31 May 1774. Alexander MONTGOMERY and Margaret Eauner. Sur. George Veale.

16 November 1792. John Joseph MORANCY and Ann Join or Jim. Sur. William Whitfield. Married 17 November by Rev. Arthur Emmerson.

14 June 1758. John MOREHOUSE and Edith Mosely. Sur. James Wood.

26 November 1770. Owen MORRIS and Elizabeth Walker. Sur. Stephen Tankard.

9 June 1767. Capt. Thomas MORRIS and Molly Bascome, dau. of Benjamin Bascome, who consents for her. Sur. Charles Butler.

1 January 1772. Thomas MORRIS and Elizabeth Poole. Sur. Howard Poole.

1 June 1768. Alexander MOSELEY and Eleanora Kelsick. Sur. Thomas Newton, Jr.

23 May 1761. Capt. Anthony MOSELEY and Dinah Scott. Sur. William Willoughby. Roderich Conner of Western Branch, guardian of Dinah, consents for her. Wit. Lewis Thelaball and Katherine Conner.

27 January 1768. Bassett MOSELEY and Rebecca Newton. Sur. Thomas Newton.

27 November 1754. Christopher MOSELEY and Eliza' Langley. Sur. Burr. Moseley.

5 December 1791. Christopher MOSELEY and Mary Butt. Sur. Henry Butt.

27 April 1757. Col. Edward Hack MOSELEY and Frances Wyllie. Sur. Samuel Boush, Jr.

25 March 1775. John MUIRHEAD and Eliza' Warner. Sur. John Brown.

18 January 1787. John MURDEN and Euphan Timberlake. Sur. Lancaster Ventriss.

28 March 1775. William MURDEN and Sarah Butt. Sur. Josiah Butt.

30 May 1791. William MURDEN and Mary Miller, dau. of Matthias Miller, who consents for her. Sur. Maximillian Murden. William makes oath Mary is of lawful age.

29 September 1758. James MURPHREE and Elizabeth Brett. Sur. Matthew Miller.

12 June 1789. George MURPHY and Nancy Cratchet of Princess Anne County. Sur. Matthias Precious. Thomas R. Walker, guardian, consents for Nancy.

13 March 1784. John MURPHY and Mrs. Mary Mackie. Sur. Matthew Wonycott. Note: Bond written Murphy, signature Murfey.

2 March 1791. Nathaniel MURPHY and Mary Poole, orphan of Nicholas Poole. Andrew Watson, surety, makes oath Mary is of lawful age.

24 June 1789. Philip MURPHY and Mrs. Elienor Mitchel. Sur. William Plume. Married 25 June 1789 by Rev. Arthur Emmerson.

9 January 1790. Christopher MURRAY and Katy Matthias. Sur. Matthew Mathias.

24 March 1767. John MURRAY and Abigail Cawson. Sur. Caleb Herbert.

30 May 1789. John MURRAY and Margaret Thompson of Portsmouth. Thomas Sturgis, surety, makes oath Margaret is of lawful age. Married 30 May 1789 by Rev. Arthur Emmerson.

5 October 1753. William MURREY and Martha Lewelling. Sur. William Newboult.

9 February 1771. Robert MUTER and Margaret Bell, dau. of John Bell. Sur. James Gilchrist. Ref: The Lower Norfolk County Virginia Antiquary.

29 September 1790. George MYARS and Martha Williamson, dau. of Margaret Williamson, who consents for her and states she was born 2 August 1768. Sur. William Grant.

7 January 1772. John NASH and Mary Odeon. Sur. Charles Mayle. John Portlock consents for Mary; no relationship stated. Wit. James Herbert.

21 April 1774. Thomas NASH and Ann Portlock, dau. of Charles Portlock. Thomas Nash, surety, makes oath Ann is of lawful age.

25 March 1754. Thomas NASH, Jr. and Mary Portlock. Sur. William Portlock.

15 October 1782. Thomas NASH, Jr. and Elizabeth Herbert. Sur. Andrew Carson.

20 June 1791. William NASH and Sophia Edwards. Thomas Edwards, surety, makes oath Sophia is of lawful age.

22 February 1723. Thomas NELSON and Mrs. Frances Tucker. Sur. John Tucker. Wit. Solomon Wilson.

30 October 1767. Benjamin NEWBOULD and Mrs. Eliza' Davis. Sur. Samuel Boush.

24 December 1791. James NEWELL and Katherine Starr. Sur. James Williams. Married 24 December by Rev. Arthur Emmerson.

2 June 1787. Edward NEWMAN and Nancy Conyers. Married by Rev. Walker Maury.

19 May 1787. William NEWMAN and Mary Denby, dau. of Elizabeth Rodman, who consents for her and states she was born 20 October 1765. Sur. Thomas Baker.

6 October 1767. Thomas NEWTON, Jr. and Martha Tucker, dau. of Joanna
Tucker, who consents for her. Sur. John Taylor. Wit. John Lee.

24 September 1774. James NICHOLSON and Lydia Cawson. Sur. Caleb
Herbert.

4 April 1744. Joshua NICHOLSON and Tabitha Lowery, dau. of James
Lowry, deceased. William Ivy, with Ann Ivy, consents for Tabitha, and
is surety.

27 August 1762. Joshua NICHOLSON and Mrs. Patience Porter. Sur. Arthur
Boush.

29 January 1760. William NICHOLSON and Mary Shields, dau. of W. Shields,
who consents for her. Sur. Alexander Bruce. Wit. Thomas Smith and
Samuell Dewbery. Note: Consent of W. Shields is addressed to "Sam'l
Boush, Schooll mate."

6 July 1773. William NICHOLSON and Lovet Tatem, orphan of Nathaniel
Tatem, deceased. Nathaniel Tatem, surety, makes oath Lovet is of lawful
age.

14 March 1785. William NICHOLSON and Mrs. Mary Parker. Sur. Archibald
Campbell.

18 August 1787. William NICHOLSON and Mrs. Isabella Manning. Sur.
Thomas Nicholas.

22 May 1732. Nathaniel NICKLIS and Mrs. _____ Mathias. Sur, John
Nicholas. Wit. William Portlock. Note: Bond written Nicklis, signature
Nicholas.

24 April 1761. Jacob NIMMO and Frances White. Sur. Gershom Nimmo.

25 June 1783. James NIMMO and Lorana Williams, dau. of Mary Williamson,
who consents for her. Sur. Jesse Jones. Wit. Robertson Mathias and
Pheneah Williamson.

23 June 1785. James NIMMO and Martha Williams. Sur. Jesse Jones. John
Williams makes oath that Martha, dau. of Charles and Aney Williams, was
born 24 January 1762.

10 September 1751. William NIMMO, Jr. and Anne Wilson. Sur. Nicholas
Slack.

2 September 1756. Joseph NISBET and White Moye. Sur. Mungo Campbell.

25 April 1787. William NIVISON and Catherine Boush. Sur. John Boush.
William is of Nansemond County. Married 25 April 1787 by Rev. Walker
Maury.

1 October 1783. Thomas NORCOT and Lydia Hodges. Sur. Wright Carney.
William Hodgis, guardian of Lydia, consents for her. Wit. John Hodges.

3 January 1789. Davis NORTON and Caroline Henrietta Tucker, dau. of
Joanna Tucker, who consents for her. Sur. G. C. Tucker.

5 April 1753. Gordon OAST and Elizabeth Dial. Sur. James Oast.

4 October 1777. Morto O'BRIEN and Joyce Edwards. Sur. Robert Brett.

15 January 1770. Charles ODEAN and Mrs. Martha Davidson. Sur. Caleb Herbert.

23 July 1789. Samuel ODIERNE and Mrs. Mary Shafer. Sur. John Northern of North Carolina.

25 October 1792. John OKLEY and Mary Mansfield. Sur. Robert Mansfield.

20 September 1764. Willoughby OLD and Martha Maning. Sur. James Webb.

7 December 1774. Malachi OLDNER and Ann Tatem. Sur. James Tatem.
Hannah Edy makes oath that Ann, dau. of Nathaniel Tatem, deceased, is of lawful age. Malachi is the son of George and Dinah Oldner.

26 June 1752. Thomas OLDNER and Sarah Wakefield. Sur. George Wakefield.

2 September 1769. John OLIFFE and Mrs. Anne Knight. Sur. George Gordon.

30 October 1784. John ORTON and Livinia Tart. Name of surety not known.

17 February 1773. David OSHEAL and Catherine Veal, dau. of George Veale, who consents for her. Sur. Samuel Boush.

8 July 1766. James OSWALL (or Oswald) and Rachel Mercer, dau. of John Mercer, Sr., who consents for her and states she was born 11 August 1743. Sur. John Mercer, Jr.

4 December 1790. John OVERTON and Frankey Taylor. Matthias Taylor, surety, makes oath Frankey, dau. of Thomas Taylor, is of lawful age.

27 October 1792. Peter OVERTON and Mary Stewart. Sur. Caleb Morgan.

26 February 1789. Edward OWENS and Mrs. Rose Elliot. Sur. James Caton.
Married 10 March 1789 by Rev. Arthur Emmerson.

18 December 1792. Edward OWENS and Elizabeth Richardson. Sur. William Richardson. Married 20 December by Rev. Arthur Emmerson.

20 May 1773. John OWENS and Sarah Wilkins. Sur. Willis Wilkins.

11 November 1774. Paul OWENS and Janet Herbert, dau. of William Herbert, who consents for her. Sur. Reubin Herbert. Wit. Charles Herbert.
Note: Bond written Owens, signature Oweins.

19 December 1787. Thomas OWENS and Mary Taylor. Sur. Jeames Taylor.

8 July 1790. Archibald PARK and Elizabeth Cotton. Sur. Archibald McGoun.

20 October 1784. William PARTRICK and Mary Holt. Sur. William Crocker.

20 December 1770. James PASTEUR and Leticy Langley. Sur. John Corprew.

4 August 1762. John PASTEUR and Abi Ballentine. Sur. Archibald Campbell.
James Pasteur consents for his son John. Wit. Richard Templeton and
Abram Wormington. Simon Portlock, guardian of Abi, consents for her.
Wit. James Cleeves and John Richardson.

7 December 1784. John PATTERSON and Elisabeth Brown. Sur. Daniel
Rothery. _____ Brown makes oath Elisabeth is of lawful age; no
relationship is stated.

8 January 1779. Michael Payne and Lydia Nicholson. Sur. Jonas Herbert.

28 April 1789. David PEARCE and Sarah Langley, orphan of James Langley.
James Langley, surety, makes oath Sarah is of lawful age.

5 July 1787. Moses Ingraham PEARCE and Mrs. Mary Chandler. Sur. Daniel
McPherson.

27 January 1784. Thomas PEARCE and Elisabeth Roberts. Sur. Lemuel
Roberts.

29 January 1770. Roger PEARSE and Teresa Boyd. Sur. John Colvill.

4 June 1755. Francis PEART and Catherine Brown. Sur. John Cann.

5 September 1767. Griffin PEART and Mrs. Eliza' Fife. Sur. Francis
Peart.

18 March 1791. Joshua PEATON and Elizabeth Shermedine, who consents for
herself. Sur. Solomon Lambert. John Shermedine makes oath Elizabeth
is of lawful age; no relationship stated.

1 November 1792. William PEATON and Betsy Benthall. Sur. Harrison
Benthall.

5 February 1780. John PEED and Ann Brannon. Sur. John Branan.

24 July 1789. Nathaniel PEED and Mary Bryan. Sur. Robert Thompson.
Married 25 July 1789 by Rev. Arthur Emmerson.

-- 1792. John PEEDE and Pattey Howard. Married by Rev. Arthur Emmerson.

3 June 1791. William PEEK and Abigail Savells. Sur. Taylor Savells.
Note: Bond written Peak, signature Peek.

6 June 1792. John PERKINS and Sally Higgins, orphan of James Higgins.
Sur. James Maning. John makes oath Sally is of lawful age.

20 December 1792. Richard PERKINS and Nancy Eastwood. Sur. William
Ward.

10 September 1787. William PERRY and Elisabeth Sikes, who consents for self.

    Note: "Sir

      The bearer Wm Perry having a inclination to enter into the married state & having no money to purchase his license with, being an old continental drummer, he has prevailed on me to give him as much as will answer this purpose: I will pay you the cost thereof on sight.

        I am yr. Obt Servt.

                Thos. Newton, Jr."

"The woman is at least thirty years old."

"Sir

  Be pleased to grant unto Wm Perry a license of marriage to yr. Humble Servt.

              her
          Elizabeth X sikes."
            mark

    Wit. Costing Sikes
       John Boush Esq.
       Clerk of Norfolk County

12 May 1789. William PERRY and Mrs. Jemimah Roach. Sur. Daniel Savell.

31 January 1787. John PETERS and Ann Whiddon, dau. of John Whiddon of Portsmouth, who consents for her. Sur. W. Graves. Wit. Euphan Corprew, Elizabeth Cunningham and William Cunningham. Married 1 February by Rev. Walker Maury.

13 August 1772. John PHILLIPS and Eliza' Lamount. Sur. Francis Miller.

31 August 1761. Thomas PHILLIPS and Margaret Hughes. Sur. Aaron Hews.

25 July 1728. John PHRIPP and Frances Mason. Sur. Solomon Wilson.

25 March 1779. Capt. Ralph PICKETT and Mary Hansford, dau. of Edward Hansford, who consents for her. Sur. Nathaniel Burgess.

8 October 1792. David PIERCE and Elizabeth Owens, orphan of William Owens. Jeremiah Cherry, surety, makes oath Elizabeth is of lawful age.

24 January 1785. Conrad Joseph PIQUET and Mrs. Jane McLacklan. Sur. Benjamin Blythe.

26 May 1784. Benjamin POLLARD and Abigail Taylor. Sur. James Taylor.

15 January 1791. John POLLOCK and Mrs. Dorothy Somerville. Sur. J. McKinnie.

8 May 1765. John POOL and Mary Carter. Sur. Robert Thompson.

6 November 1779. John POOL and Elisabeth Portlock. Sur. James Leitch.

1 December 1792. John POOL and Molly Wray. Sur. Lemuel Roberts.

25 August 1791. John POOLE, Jr. and Mrs. Mary Hill. Sur. John Pool.

3 April 1732. Richard POOLE and Mrs. Ann Butt. Sur. Lemuel Nicholson.

19 November 1772. Robert POOLE and Mary Sikes. Sur. John Boushell.

19 March 1772. Thomas POOLE and Eliza' Riddick. Sur. James Murphree.

8 November 1779. Elijah POOPE and Mary Butt. Sur. Cartwright Butt.

19 May 1785. Robert PORTEL and Mary Griggs. Sur. Henry Ballance.

20 February 1765. Capt. David PORTER and Agnis Veal, dau. of George Veale, who consents for her. Sur. Matthew Godfrey. Wit. Beckey Porter and Samuel Veale.

2 July 1770. David PORTER and Ann Wonycott, dau. of Nicholas Wonycott, who consents for her. Sur. Matthew Godfrey.

6 May 1731. William PORTER and Kezia Cawson. Surety not named.

11 April 1738. William PORTER and Patience Wright. Sur. Lemuel Nicholson.

30 October 1782. William PORTER and Elizabeth Luke, dau. of Isaac Luke. Sur. Paul Dale Duke.

26 January 1742. John PORTLOCK and Abiah Portlock. Sur. Edward Portlock.

13 August 1777. John PORTLOCK, Jr. and Elizabeth Nash. Sur. Thomas Nash, Jr.

11 January 1787. John PORTLOCK and Lydia Herbert. Sur. Caleb Herbert. Married 16 January 1787 by Rev. Walker Maury.

19 September 1754. Jonathan PORTLOCK and Mary Bevan. Sur. George Poole.

10 April 1779. Thomas PORTLOCK and Catherine Hartford. Sur. Lemuel Portlock. Nathaniel Denby, guardian of Catherine, consents for her.

24 December 1790. Jesse POULTON and Mary Macneil. Sur. Philip Ritter. John Mackneil consents for Capt. Jessey Poulton to marry his dau. Mary.

16 January 1778. Jermiah POWELL and Mrs. Ann Wright. Sur. James Nichols.

9 July 1785. Thomas POWELL and Mrs. Sarah Grimes. Sur. John Isdall.

21 May 1792. Thomas POWELL and Ludwell Harrison, orphan of John Harrison. John Hollowell, surety, makes oath Ludwell is of lawful age.

28 February 1787. William POWELL and Mrs. Elisa' Creech. Sur. Thomas Powell.

5 October 1792. Samuel POYNER and Selah Cherry Marcer or Mcrea, dau. of John Cherry, who consents for her. Sur. James Burgess. Wit. William Baker. Married 10 October by Rev. Arthur Emmerson.

7 July 1755. William PRATA and Courtnay Edmonds. Sur. Francis Peart. Alis Ivy makes oath that Courtnay, the daughter of Mary Richards, is of lawful age.

20 May 1783. John PRESCOTT and Elizabeth Wadlington. Sur. Richard Bickardick.

10 November 1792. John PRETER and Mrs. Mary Robinson. Sur. William Williams. Note: Bond written Prater, signature Preter.

19 November 1785. William PRICE and Mary Banks. Sur. Thomas Wakefield.

19 June 1778. William PRITCHET and Mary Eastwood, dau. of Elisha Eastwood. Sur. John Morris. Ref: The Lower Norfolk County Virginia Antiquary.

4 July 1771. Paul PROBY and Mary Pugh, dau. of Edward Pugh. Sur. Paul Loyall. Ref: The Lower Norfolk County Virginia Antiquary.

25 November 1791. Jonathan PROCTER and Elisabeth Cooper. Sur. Elias Boyer. Jonathan makes oath Elisabeth is of lawful age.

13 April 1770. Dickerson PRYOR and Mrs. Frances Frazier. Sur. Hardress Waller.

19 June 1755. Edward PUGH and Lucy Calvert. Sur. Alexander Ross.

10 February 1792. Henry PULLEN and Celia Jolliff, orphan of James Jolliff. Willis Wingate, surety, makes oath Celia is of lawful age.

22 July 1764. Joseph PULLETT and Mary Sills. Sur. Philip Carbery.

21 June 1790. Henry PULLIN and Elisabeth Smith. Sur. Hezekiah Taylor.

17 December 1792. John PULLIN and Peggy Powell. Sur. John Carney. Note: Bond written Pulling, signature Pullin.

5 October 1779. John QUARLES and Mary Hudson. Sur. John Smith.

23 September 1761. James RAE and Abigail Conner, dau. of William Conner, who consents for her. Sur. Samuel Boush. Wit. John Ross and Moses Richardson.

29 October 1761. James RAMSEY and Ann Ballard. Sur. Samuel Boush.

27 June 1787. James RAMSEY and Mrs. Margaret Boush. Sur. John Lightfoot. Married 28 June 1787 by Rev. Walker Maury.

5 January 1757. Doctor John RAMSEY and Mary Hutchings, dau. of John Hutchings, who consents for her. Sur. John Hutchings, Jr. Wit. John Tucker.

5 September 1767. John RANDLE and Elizabeth Wilkins. Sur. Daniel Barraud.

16 June 1792. William RANDOLPH and Charity Best, orphan of Henry Best. Archibald Bruce, surety, makes oath Charity is of lawful age.

14 March 1785. Willis RANDOLPH and Prudence White, dau. of Sarah White, who consents for her and makes oath she was born 15 June 1760. Sur. David Fentress.

23 May 1791. William READ and Mrs. Elizabeth Browning. Sur. William Burn.

30 September 1792. William READ and Mrs. Ann Gale. Sur. Stephen Makins. Note: Bond written Reed, signature Read. Married by Rev. Arthur Emmerson.

21 December 1782. George REARDON and Ann Walker. Sur. John Branan.

23 March 1765. Thomas REDMAN and Mary Gibson. Sur. Thomas King.

19 July 1791. John REED and Lucy Cooke. Willis Hanbury, surety, makes oath Lucy is of lawful age. Married 31 August by Rev. Arthur Emmerson, who records "John Read and July Cook."

14 December 1789. William REED and Mrs. Ann Wormsley. Sur. Robert Walmsley.

21 August 1790. William REED and Alice Wilson, orphan of Malachi Wilson, deceased. Sur. George D. Corprew. John Smith Younger makes oath that Alice is of lawful age. Note: Another Marriage Bond of William Reed and Alice Wilson is dated 20 September 1790.

7 November 1787 or 1788. David REES and Mary Rothery. Married by Rev. Arthur Emmerson.

26 October 1785. Powell REINS and Ann Nicholson, dau. of Mary Sparrow, who consents for her. Sur. James Dyson.

20 December 1782. George REVELEY and Martha Lakeland. Sur. Richard Jones. Ref: The Lower Norfolk County Virginia Antiquary.

18 December 1789. Patrick RICE and Drusilla Nichols. Sur. Robert Boush. Married 18 December 1789 by Rev. Arthur Emmerson.

15 January 1790. James RICHARDSON and Frankey Culpeper. Sur. John Culpeper.

6 March 1792. Jeremiah RICHARDSON and Elizabeth Emberson, orphan of James Emberson. Sur. George Smith. Jeremiah makes oath Elizabeth is of lawful age.

19 September 1772. John RICHARDSON and Eliza' Herbert. Sur. Nathaniel Young. John Whiddon, guardian of Eliza', consents for her. Wit. Matthew Jackson and Mary Harding.

6 January 1792. Thomas RICHARDSON and Elizabeth Coffield, dau. of Willis Coffield, deceased. Robert Culpepper, surety, makes oath Elizabeth is of lawful age.

22 March 1785. William RICHARDSON and Margaret Culpeper, dau. of William and Mary Culpepper, who consent for her. Sur. Thomas Richardson.

9 June 1784. Millison RITEN or Biten: see Millerson Wrighton.

15 October 1774. Thomas RITSON and Martha Willoughby. Sur. John Willoughby.

17 March 1784. Philip RITTER and Mary Willoughby, dau. of Thomas and Mary Willoughby, who consent for her. Sur. John Barrett. Wit. William Willoughby.

2 March 1767. Joseph RIVES and Margaret Hutton. Sur. John Rodman.

23 January 1790. Joseph ROACH and Dinah Williams. Thomas Nicholas, surety, makes oath that Dinah, dau. of William Williams, is of lawful age.

17 February 1791. Antonio Penez ROBALLO and Mrs. Nancy Hamilton. Sur. Thomas Driskell. A Nancy Hamilton requests a marriage license for Mrs. Nancy Hamilton! Wit. Edm. Warriner. Married 20 February by Rev. Arthur Emmerson.

29 March 1759. James ROBE and Elizabeth Gordon. Sur. Robert Mercciare.

19 June 1752. John ROBE and Mrs. Mary Fife. Sur. John Cann. Wit. George Pool.

7 February 1759. Butts ROBERTS and Sarah Church. Sur. Simon Wilson.

22 December 1781. Lemuel ROBERTS and Ann Shore. Sur. Goldsbery Hacket.

29 October 1768. Thomas ROBERTS and Frances Calvert. Sur. Archibald Campbell.

16 March 1753. William ROBERTS and Ann Jennings. Sur. Willis Scott. Note: Thomas Scott was appt. gd. to Ann in Elizabeth City County Court.

17 July 1777. William ROBERTS and Mary Veale. Sur. Samuel Veale.

2 June 1791. William ROBERTS and Mary Johnson, orphan of Maner Johnson. William Spillman, surety, makes oath Mary is of lawful age. Married by Rev. Arthur Emmerson.

9 August 1732. The Rev'd Mr. Moses ROBERTSON and Mary Willoughby. Sur. Solomon Wilson.

28 October 1774. George ROBINSON and Eliza' Bayne. Sur. John Bayne.

8 October 1792. William ROGERS and Peggy Butt, dau. of Peter Butt, deceased. Sur. William G. Knight. Henning Butt makes oath Peggy is of lawful age; no relationship stated.

3 February 1774. Andrew RONALD and Mary Fry. Sur. Robert Fry.

1 March 1785. William RONALD and Anne Waller. Sur. John Bowdoin. Robert Waller consents for Anne; no relationship stated.

17 March 1785. Daniel ROSE and Judith Norcut. Sur. Richard Powell.

8 October 1791. William ROSE and Sally Singleton, orphan of John Singleton. Sur. Joshua Woodhouse. William makes oath Sally is of lawful age.

6 September 1779. Christopher ROSS and Mary Marshall. Sur. Thomas Marshall.

28 December 1779. John ROSS and Lydia Price, dau. of Thomas Price, who consents for her. Sur. John Freeman.

3 September 1771. Charles ROTHERY and Eliza' Standey. Sur. Robert Steed. Ref: The Lower Norfolk County Virginia Antiquary.

9 February 1760. Daniel ROTHERY and Ann Rothery. Sur. Henery Rothery.

25 May 1785. Daniel ROTHERY and Clavy Stark. Sur. Boling Stark. Hillary Moseley consents for his ward, Daniel.

14 June 1764. Henry ROTHERY and Mrs. Mary Godfrey. Sur. Matthew Rothery.

4 April 1763. Matthew ROTHERY and Mary Orange, dau. of William Orange of Norfolk Borough, who consents for her and is surety.

12 September 1791. Robert ROUTH and Sally Owens. Sur. John Owens.

28 April 1784. Charles RUDDER and Margaret McCoy. Sur. Thomas McCoy.

16 April 1787. John RUDDER and Mrs. Charity Whitehurst. Sur. Charles Rudder, Sr.

16 July 1760. John RUMBERG and Rebecca Pearson. Sur. Robert Moorie.

16 February 1783. Elihu RUSSELL and Mary Herbert. Sur. Thomas Herbert.

5 September 1775. Francis RUSSELL and Elizabeth Dunn. Sur. John Dunn.

17 November 1790. Thomas RYAN and Catharine Mathers. Sur. Hugh Donnell. Catharine makes oath that she is of lawful age.

26 June 1792. Pierre Louis SAFFRAY and Mary Eddenton. Sur. Henry Collins. Note: Bond written Peter Lewis Saffray, signature Pierre Louis Saffray.

5 March 1790. Penn Townsend SALE and Ann Conyers. Sur. John Brown. Married 6 July 1790 by Rev. Arthur Emmerson.

1 June 1792. John Murray SAMUEL and Mary Ann Smith. Sur. Thomas Allan. John makes oath Mary Ann is of lawful age.

1 August 1785. Samuel SANDIFORD and Polly Fells. Sur. George Cameron. Nancy Mills makes oath that Polly is of the Town of Portsmouth and is of lawful age.

9 January 1789. Daniel SANFORD and Martha Maund. Sur. Thomas Newton, Jr.

3 July 1790. William SAUNDERS and Elizabeth Singleton. John Singleton, surety, makes oath Elizabeth is the orphan of Anthony Singleton and is of lawful age.

20 October 1785. Daniel SAVELLS and Frances Cherry. Sur. David Manning. Daniel makes oath that Frances, the dau. of Caleb Cherry, is of lawful age.

27 May 1734. John SAYER and Elizabeth Gwin. Sur. Benjamin Gwin.

16 April 1789. Joseph SCALF and Lydia Stewart. Sur. John Stewart.

1 June 1789. John SCOTT and Mrs. Rebecca Harvey. Sur. James Wear. Married 2 June 1789 by Rev. Arthur Emmerson.

2 December 1752. Richard SCOTT and Rebecca Portlock. Sur. George Abyvon.

15 July 1778. Tenant SCOTT and Rebecca Wonycott. Sur. Matthew Godfrey.

15 August 1727. Thomas SCOTT and Martha Scott. Sur. Solomon Wilson.

15 December 1758. William SCOTT and Prudence Dale. Sur. Paul Kingston.

16 November 1790. Nicholas Shacklock and Sally McPherson. Sur. William Hannah.

17 August 1771. John SHAW and Mrs. Mary Arnott. Sur. John Ewing.

24 June 1790. James SHAY and Mrs. Courtney Moore. Sur. George Reveley.

18 December 1790. James SHAY and Mrs. Molly Hainsworth. Sur. Robert McCredie.

29 January 1772. John SHEDDEN and Molly Goodrich. Sur. John Goodrich.

30 August 1767. Robert SHEDDEN and Agatha Wells Goodrich. Sur. John Goodrich.

20 December 1792. John SHEE and Elizabeth Rosseter. Sur. Michael Bourke. John makes oath that both he and Elizabeth are of lawful age.

15 November 1790. Amos E. SHEPHERD and Fanny Shields. Sur. John Corprew.

20 January 1769. Solomon SHEPHERD, Jr. and Elizabeth Osheal. Sur. David Osheal.

2 September 1767. Thomas SHEPHERD and Barthiah Etheredge, dau. of Amos Etheredge, who consents for her. Sur. William Crawford Conner. Wit. Thomas Edwards and Bithathae Veale.

No date, probably 1789. John SHERMEDINE and Abby Wilson. Sur. John Lambert.

5 September 1783. John SHIELDS and Jennet Hughes. Sur. David Leitch.

20 October 1787. John SHIELDS and Frances Ballentine. Married by Rev. Walker Maury.

11 August 1773. Mathew SHIELDS and Sarah Corprew. Sur. John Corprew.

21 April 1790. Mason SHIPWASH and Martha Hall. Sur. John Stewart. Ann Lane makes oath that Martha, orphan of Thomas Hall, is of lawful age. She also makes oath that Mason, son of Thomas Shipwash, is of lawful age.

20 April 1782. George SHORE and Mrs. Hannah Volum. Sur. Thomas Sterling.

3 June 1771. John SHORE and Ann Benn, dau. of James Benn. Sur. John Lee. Ref: The Lower Norfolk County Virginia Antiquary.

5 September 1792. Ivy SIKES and Catherin Miller. Edward Miller, surety, makes oath Catherin is of lawful age.

18 October 1792. James SIKES and Franky Parsons. Sur. Willis Parsons.

25 December 1793. Josiah SIKES and Mrs. Lovey Bentel. Sur. David Dennis.

17 December 1792. Stephen SIKES and Margaret Moore. Sur. Zachariah Nichols. Married by Rev. Arthur Emmerson who records date as 22 November 1792 and who says Mary Moore.

12 July 1784. Thomas SILBAY and Mary Brown. Sur. Thomas Duffe. Mary makes oath she is of lawful age.

20 September 1790. David SILVESTER and Frances Bartee. Sur. Thomas Bartee.

24 September 1787. James SIMMONS and Mrs. Mary Wilder. Sur. William Holly. Married 24 September 1787 by Rev. Walker Maury.

26 July 1762. Southward SIMMONS and Martha Wallis, dau. of John Wallis, who consents for her. Sur. Malachi Wilson, Jr. and John Walis.

3 December 1752. William SIMMONS and Mrs. Sarah Stant or Hant. Sur. Solomon Lambert.

28 February 1765. Richard SIMMS and Susanah Archer. Sur. Edward Archer.

7 October 1791. George SIMONS and Ann Dudley, orphan of William Dudley. William Dudley, surety, makes oath Ann is of lawful age.

12 September 1760. Thomas SIMPSON and Ann Dale, dau. of Daniel Dale, who consents for her. Sur. George Collins. Wit. William Dale.

20 August 1783. John SINGLETON and Sarah Dison. Sur. William Willoughby.

17 August 1772. William SKINKER and Mary Pullet. Sur. Nathaniel Boush.

4 April 1778. William SKINNER and Frances Tomer. Wit. Thomas Tomer.

4 January 1760. Josias SLACK and Mary Warden. Sur. Lamuel Warden. Wit. Thomas Holstead and Holstead Hollowell.

29 April 1728. Nicholas SLACK and Eliza Stewart. Sur. Solomon Wilson. Wit. Ann Bouon.

3 January 1767. William SLEY and Sarah Lancaster. Sur. James Smith.

17 March 1785. Andrew SMITH and Mrs. Mary Wright. Sur. Thomas Allan. Wit. John Kid and Edward Hansford. Note: A Mary Wright consents.

17 April 1762. Charles SMITH and Elizabeth Jolliff, dau. of Richard Jolliff, who consents for her. Sur. James Jolliff. Wit. Solomon Smith.

23 January 1790. Charles SMITH and Betty Hanbury. Jesse Hanbury makes oath that Betty is the orphan of Caleb Hanbury and is surety.

22 May 1787. George SMITH and Mary Brown. Sur. Ivy Brown.

20 January 1759. Henry SMITH and Sarah Miller. Sur. Rasha (Horatio) Butt.

7 September 1765. James SMITH and Elizabeth Gregory. Sur. Benjamin Collett.

13 May 1762. John SMITH and Penelope Talbutt. Sur. Thomas Talbot. John Hutchings consents for John; no relationship stated.

13 September 1764. John SMITH and Priscilla Milner. Sur. Richard Knight.

14 April 1789. John SMITH and Eupan Corprew, dau. of John Corprew, who consents for her. Sur. Hillary Butt. Wit. Thomas Bressie.

21 April 1790. Joshua SMITH and Keziah Savills, dau. of Daniel Savills, who consents for her. Sur. Henry Smith.

9 November 1790. Richard SMITH and Mrs. Elizabeth Johnston. Sur. John Drinane.

16 October 1765. Samuel SMITH and Mary Foreman, dau. of Jermiah Foreman, who consents for her. Sur. Thomas Leak.

22 March 1790. Simon SMITH and Mrs. Polly Wallace. Isaiah Butt makes oath that Polly is the widow of Roger Wallace and he is surety.

4 November 1762. Solomon SMITH and Prudence Wilson. Sur. Josiah Wilson.

30 September 1765. Solomon SMITH and Elizabeth Wilson. Sur. Malachi Wilson.

14 November 1752. William SMITH and Ann Cleeves. Sur. James Cleeves. Samuel Boush, Jr. Test. for John Cleeves. Thomas Whitford Test. for William Smith. Wit. Charles Smith.

21 May 1765. William SMITH and Sarah Stammers. Sur. William Freeman.

25 April 1789. William SMITH and Nancy Hodges. Sur. Mason Hodges.

6 January 1779. John SMITHSON and Mary Hartfoot. Sur. Maximilian Grimes. John Peek makes oath that Mary is of lawful age.

17 March 1790. William Robinson SMYTH and Martha Taylor. Sur. Jeames Taylor.

21 November 1782. Christopher SNAIL and Fanny McCloud. Sur. James McCloud.

20 September 1785. Henry SNAIL and Mrs. Fanny McCloud. Sur. Francis Snail.

14 September 1763. Capt. Thomas SNALE and Eliza' Ivy, dau. of William Ivy, Sr., who consents for her. Sur. Matthias Miller.

5 January 1754. George SNOW and Mary Morisson. Sur. Peter Dale.

30 October 1759. Samuel SOUTHERLAND and Ann Watkins. Sur. John Southerland.

23 December 1791. Caleb SPANN and Nancy Brown. Sur. Stephen Hopkins. Caleb makes oath he was appointed guardian of Nancy by the Court of Princess Anne County.

23 December 1773. Henry SPARROW and Elizabeth Tucker. Sur. John Whiddon.

4 January 1773. James SPARROW and Mrs. Mary Hunter. Sur. William Sparrow.

7 September 1778. Peter SPARROW and Ruth Wooldridge. Sur. David Ballentine.

28 May 1784. Richard SPARROW and Mrs. Margaret Wilson. Sur. Maxin Marley.

4 January 1792. John SPEIRS and Ann Kite, dau. of Amos Kite. Isaiah Butt, surety, makes oath Ann is of lawful age.

2 April 1729. John SPENCER and Mary McDowell. Sur. Charles Portlock.

22 August 1784. Ralph SPENCER and Elisabeth Smith, who makes oath she is of lawful age. Sur. Francis Edwards.

11 October 1785. James Harris SPRAGUE and Hannah Cowper. Sur. John Drinane.

21 February 1792. Samuel STAFFORD and Elizabeth Ivy. Sur. James Smith. Married 24 February by Rev. Arthur Emmerson.

3 November 1752. Horatio STAMMERS and Sarah Drury. Sur. Arthur Moseley. Note: Bond written Horatio, signature Horasha.

22 January 1790. John STEELE and Sarah Lamb. Sur. Samuel Hopkins.

19 June 1769. Robert STEELE and Mrs. Sarah Cann. Sur. Robert Burns.

18 October 1779. Thomas STELLINGS and Mrs. Peggy Smith. Sur. Lionel Baker.

16 June 1785. Thomas STEPHENSON and Elisabeth Volume. Sur. George Shore.

4 February 1790. Robert STEVENS and Mrs. Molly Hill. Sur. Andrew Leary.

14 February 1772. Andrew STEVENSON and Alice Grear. Sur. William Simpson.

9 February 1775. Daniel STEWART and Sarah Butler. No surety named.

13 September 1792. Henry STEWART and Sarah Manning. Josiah Nichols, Sr. makes oath Sarah is of lawful age.

8 June 1789. John STEWART and Mrs. Elisabeth Maund. Sur. William Southerlin.

24 December 1744. Joseph STEWART and Julian Church. Sur. Thomas Corprew.

5 July 1744. Robert STEWART and Abiah Church. Sur. Joseph Stewart.

23 September 1784. Robert STEWART and Sealey Barr, dau. of Robard Barr, who consents for her. Sur. John Laycock. Wit. William Booker.

28 September 1784. Thomas STEWART and Mrs. Franky Kay, who consents for self. Sur. Samuel Hodges.

11 March 1779. Jonathan STOKES and Elisabeth Etheridge. Sur. Richard McCoy.

4 January 1791. Thomas STOKES and Mary Portlock, orphan of Seth Portlock. Charles McCoy, surety, makes oath Mary is of lawful age.

30 September 1752. John STREIP and Mary Breadey. Sur. Terence Wadick.

24 May 1764. John STREIP and Margaret Kingston. Sur. George Brown.

12 October 1772. John SUMMERILL and Esther Jenkins, grandau. of Mary Meech, who consents for her. Sur. Richard Bickardick.

20 January 1759. John SUTHERLAND and Eliza' Herbert, dau. of Thomas Herbert, who consents for her. Sur. Goodrich Boush.

7 February 1763. Capt. John SUTHERLAND and Celia Brickell, dau. of John Brickell. Sur. John Brickell.

11 December 1756. Asbury SUTTON and Mary Burdess. Surety not named.

14 February 1728/9. Lazarus SWEENY and Eliza' Wilson. Sur. Willis Wilson.

20 August 1778. Jacob SWIFT and Ann Franks. Sur. Thomas Hall.

30 March 1782. Augustine TABB and Mrs. Hannah Phripp. Sur. Alexander Moseley.

17 May 1777. John TABB and Eliza' Talbutt. Sur. Robert Langley.

6 April 1778. Solomon Butt TALBOT and Mary Tabb, dau. of William Tabb. Sur. John Hughes. Ref: The Lower Norfolk County Virginia Antiquary.

14 January 1755. Isaac TALBUTT and Eliza' Langley. Sur. John Williamson.

19 September 1751. Shadrack TALBUTT and Sarah Talbutt. Sur. John Guy.

9 March 1792. Francis TARRANT and Elizabeth Sweney. Sur. Cha:s. Boush.

24 October 1787. John TART and Mary Taylor. Sur. Arthur Taylor.

8 March 1790. John TART and Mrs. Mary Smith. Sur. Ivy Brown. John makes oath he is of lawful age.

17 December 1787. Robert TART and Esther Wilson. Sur. William Bunting. Robert makes oath Esther is of lawful age.

9 July 1782. James TATEM and Polly Williamson. Sur. Nathaniel Tatem.

7 November 1743. John TATEM and Anne Wright, dau. of Stephen Wright, who consents for her. Sur. Samuel Boush. Wit. William Craford and Lemuel Langley.

7 November 1772. John TATEM and Eliza' Wright Carney. Sur. Barnaby Carney.

30 March 1774. John TATEM, Sr. and Abey Smith. Sur. John Archer.

13 December 1743. Nathaniel TATEM, Jr. and Prudence Wilson, dau. of Major James Wilson, Sr., who consents for her. Sur. John Taylor. Wit. Nicholas Wonycutt and George Abyvon.

12 February 1755. Nathaniel TATEM and Dinah Nash, dau. of Thomas Nash, who consents for her. Sur. Trimigin Tatem. Wit. William Portlock, Jr. and Annas Portlock.

29 October 1773. Nathaniel TATEM and Rebecca Portlock. Sur. John Portlock.

22 February 1785. Nathaniel TATEM and Elisabeth Wright. Willis Strator, surety, makes oath Elisabeth is of lawful age.

19 December 1778. Solomon TATEM and Sarah Carney, dau. of Sarah Carney, Sr. Sur. Richard Barr. Ref: The Lower Norfolk County Virginia Antiquary.

24 December 1791. Arthur TAYLER and Mrs. Rebecca Archer. Sur. Wilson Smith. Married 5 January 1792 by Rev. Arthur Emmerson.

28 April 1763. Alexander TAYLOR and Elizabeth Sparrow. Sur. James Taylor.

7 May 1758. Archibald TAYLOR and Louisa Richard, dau. of Andre Richard, who consents for her. Sur. Nathaniel Fife.

21 June 1783. Arthur TAYLOR and Phebe Eastwood. Sur. John Lockhart.

10 November 1792. Hezekiah TAYLOR and Mrs. Sarah Wildair. Sur. William Crocker.

15 April 1761. James TAYLOR and Alice Smith. Sur. Charles Smith. Wit. John Phripps, Jr. and Fernelia Elligood.

28 May 1766. John TAYLOR and Sarah Tucker. Sur. Robert Tucker, Sr.

27 April 1774. John TAYLOR and Mary Rhonald. Sur. Alexander Gordon.

28 July 1792. John TAYLOR and Kezia Ellis. Sur. Samuel Ellis. Married 2 August by Rev. Arthur Emmerson.

31 January 1768. Peter TAYLOR and Margaret Wallace. Sur. Andrew Bathingall.

18 March 1789. Purnell TAYLOR and Mary Eastwood. Sur. Severn Kellum. Enos Eastwood, guardian of Mary, makes consent for her. Wit. Peter Kellum and Willis Eastwood.

7 March 1784. Richard TAYLOR and Elizabeth Bacon. Married by Rev. Edward Mintz.

26 September 1771. Robert TAYLOR and Sarah Barraud, dau. of David Barraud. Sur. Hector MacAlester. Ref: The Lower Norfolk County Virginia Antiquary.

16 May 1774. James THELABALL and Anne Wishart. Sur. John Griffin. William Wishart, brother, and guardian of Anne, consents for her.

11 February 1737/8. John THOMAS and Eliza' Oagely. Sur. John Drury.

23 October 1790. Nathan THOMAS and Mrs. Mary Ward. Sur. Edmund Warriner. Married 23 October 1790 by Rev. Arthur Emmerson.

24 December 1790. William THOMAS and Judy Beckley. Sur. Francis Beckley.

8 May 1762. Christopher THOMPSON and Mrs. Margaret Ritch. Sur. John Kay.

20 January 1763. Isaac THOMPSON and Mrs. Prudence Scott. Sur. Richard Butt.

8 June 1763. Robert THOMPSON and Isabel Franks. Sur. John Vandervert.

15 August 1754. Thomas THOMPSON and Sophia Kinner. Sur. Richard Kelsick.

16 December 1762. Alexander THOMSON and Mary Ross. Sur. John Ross, Sr.

19 June 1787. Joshua THORNTON and Nancy Wilkins. Sur. John Branan, Jr.

9 August 1782. Francis THOROWGOOD and Mary Easter. Sur. Malbone Shelton.

22 March 1787. John THOROWGOOD and Bridgett Guy. Sur. John Guy.

26 March 1791. John THOURAN and Ann Smith. Sur. A. Slaughter. Married
26 March by Rev. Arthur Emmerson.
Note: "Sir

> A French gentleman in a consumption from which there is no
> prospect of recovery, is desirous of marrying a lady that she
> may enjoy his property after his decease. If any formality is
> necessary to obtain a license for that purpose, please to
> acquaint the bearer, who waits on you for me. I will be Mr.
> John Thourons (the gentleman in question) security.

> N.B. The lady   I am Sir your most hble Servt.
> is from Baltimore,
> her name Ann Smith,   A Slaughter
> about 40 years of age.   March 27, 1791
> I beg Mr. Boush will throw as few
> obstacles in the way as possible."   Note difference in dates.

27 April 1744. Thomas TIBBS and Martha Tomouth. Sur. Lemuel Wilson.

2 August 1791. Elihu TIMMENS and Nancy Pulling. Sur. Richard Bacon.

26 April 1783. Charles TOMER and Nancy But---(ran off page). Sur.
Geo. Thos. Hall.

17 November 1770. Samuel TOMLINSON and Ann Pearce, dau. of John Peirce,
who consents for her. Sur. John Dunn. Wit. William Bean and Sarah
Star.

26 November 1784. William TOMLINSON and Ann Redd. Christopher Snail,
surety, makes oath Ann is of lawful age.

20 September 1790. David TOPPING and Mrs. Ann Bailey. Sur. Daniel
McPherson. Married 21 September 1790 by Rev. Thomas Armistead.

15 March 1792. William TOWNES and Ann Godwin. Sur. Thomas Shepherd.
Note: Bond written Towns, signature Townes.

31 August 1784. Dormand TOWNSHEND and Mrs. Lydia Hawkins or Hankins.
Sur. William Higinbotham. Note: Dormand Townshend also spelled Doman
Towson.

28 November 1772. Champion TRAVIS and Elizabeth Boush. Sur. Samuel Boush.

21 May 1785. John TRIMBLE and Lydia Tatem. George Wilson, guardian of Lydia, consents for her and is surety.

16 April 1791. John TRIMBLE and Elizabeth Wigley. Sur. Henry Sharp. John makes oath Elizabeth is of lawful age.

17 February 1765. Henry TUCKER and Mary Cole. Sur. Samuel Boush.

29 August 1750. Robert TUCKER and Elizabeth Cleeves. Sur. James Cleeves.

26 July 1764 (date of consent). Robert TUCKER and Fanny McPherson. Robert Tucker consents for his son Robert and makes oath that he was born 24 September 1741 and Fanny was born July 1741. Archibald Campbell makes oath Fanny is of lawful age.

7 October 1778. William TUCKER and Mrs. Elizabeth Richardson. Sur. Robert Tucker. Ref: The Lower Norfolk County Virginia Antiquary.

15 September 1792. Willis TUCKER and Nancy Tartt. Sur. Thomas Tartt.

17 March 1779. Willoughby TUCKER and Margaret Culpepper, dau. of John Culpepper and wife (not named). Sur. John Batchelor. Wit. John Culpepper and L. Culpepper.

14 January 1789. John TUMBLIN and Sarah Bully. John Bully, surety, consents for Sarah; no relationship stated. Wit. William Benthal.

14 January 1784. Henry TURNER and Martha Wood. Sur. Matthew Douglass.

24 November 1787. George VALENTINE and Dinah Sparrow. Sur. Isaac Jackson. Rev. Walker Maury states he married the above couple on 14 November 1787 and that they are mullatos (mulattoes).

4 June 1761. George VEALE, Jr. and Mary Morgan. Sur. Charles Smith. Note: "Morgan/Mary was born October 15, 1738 & entered on the E. R. P. according to the manuscript shown me, whereof this is a true copy. 4 June 1761.   Charles Smith"

15 November 1763. Capt. Thomas VEALE and Bathia(h) Edwards. Sur. William Dale.

28 June 1787. William VEALE and Jane Skinner. Sur. Richard Bickardick.

1 April 1767. William VERLING and Elizabeth Conner, dau. of William Conner, who consents for her. Sur. Henry Gifford. Wit. Isaac (torn) oore.

11 August 1784. Francis VERMILION and Anne Williams. Married by Rev. Arthur Emmerson.

28 August 1779. Joseph VESEY and Fanny Dameron. Sur. Lemuel Langley.

8 May 1782. Joseph VESEY and Keziah Jones. Sur. Lemuel Langley.

13 May 1772. James VICKERS and Alby Farr, a free woman. Sur. John McNeal. Note: Norfolk 14th, 1772.
To Samuel Boush Esq.
These are to certify that Alby Farr is a free woman and noways Engaged to any Person or Contracted and is aged to the years above twenty one. As Witness My Hand The Day of Date Above Mentioned.

her
Test. John McNeal.   Alse X Stevenson
mark

26 January 1787. Thomas VICKERS and Sarah Denby. Sur. Mills Mansfield.

17 January 1792. James WADDEY and Catharine Mahanes, orphan of John Mahanes. James Waddey, surety, makes oath Catharine is of lawful age.

30 December 1785. William WAINRIGHT and Lydia Grimes. Surety not named.

10 May 1792. George WAKEFIELD and Thamer Cooper, orphan of Samuel Cooper. James Cooper, surety, makes oath Thamer is of lawful age.

17 August 1764. Thomas WAKEFIELD and Sarah Dunn. Sur. Christopher Bustin.

16 March 1792. Thomas WAKEFIELD and Mrs. Nancy Haire. Sur. Thomas Holdness.

23 April 1789. William WAKEFIELD and Elizabeth Eastwood, orphan of Willis Eastwood. Miles King makes oath that Elizabeth is of lawful age and he is surety.

21 December 1782. William WALKE and Mary Calvert. Sur. Anthony Walke. William is the son of Mary Walke. Ref: The Lower Norfolk County Virginia Antiquary.

6 November 1723. Jacob WALKER and Courtney Tucker. Sur. John Tucker. Wit. Paul Portlock.

26 August 1766. James WALKER and Mrs. Mary Duff. Sur. James Leitch.

8 December 1785. John WALKER and Mrs. Venus Drewry. Sur. Benjamin Wilson.

22 September 1792. Jesse WALLACE and Phebe Williams. Sur. James Stewart.

13 February 1778. Thomas WALLACE and Elizabeth Stewart, dau. of John Stewart. Sur. Willis Leak. Ref: The Lower Norfolk County Virginia Antiquary.

19 June 1765. Hardress WALLER and Anne Godfrey. Sur. John Godfrey.

25 January 1791. John WALLER and Polly Miller, orphan of Bateman Miller. Sur. Edward Miller. John makes oath Polly is of lawful age.

3 June 1758. Robert WALLER and Mason Wilson. Sur. Samuel Boush, Jr.

2 June 1785. Robert WALMSLEY and Rhoda Cooper, dau. of Daniel Cooper. James Cooper, surety, consents for Rhoda and makes oath she is of lawful age.

28 July 1791. Robert WALMSLY and Comfort Kellum. Sur. Thomas Walmsly. Comfort makes oath she is of lawful age. Note: Bond written Walmsley, signature Walmsly.

23 April 1754. John WALSH and Patience Davis. Sur. Richard Taylor.

11 December 1783. Benjamin WARD(or Word) and Elisabeth Godfrey. Sur. Obadiah Mason.

15 December 1785. Caleb WARD and Mrs. Maron Taylor. Sur. William Jones.

2 July 1792. James WARD and Mrs. Mary Ross. Sur. George Godfrey.

31 January 1784. Peter WARD and Mary Cooper. Sur. Robert Anderson. Mrs. Mary Recuba makes oath that her dau., Mary, is of lawful age and consents for her.

23 April 1787. William WARD and Mary Burgess, dau. of John Burgess, who consents for her. Sur. William Ward (Sr.?). Wit. Daniel Godfrey, Benjamin Ward and John Burgis.

26 May 1785. James WARDEN, Jr. and Mary Parke. Sur. John Valentine.

31 May 1784. Joseph WARDEN and Mrs. Rebecca Blades. Sur. Richard Jarvis.

4 January 1771. Bayley WARREN and Elizabeth Dickenson of Princess Anne County and dau. of Thomas Dickenson, deceased. Ref: The Lower Norfolk County Virginia Antiquary.

23 April 1792. James WARREN and Mrs. Mary Ward. Sur. William Whitfield.

28 November 1778. John WARREN and Frances Childers. Sur. R. Taylor. Ref: The Lower Norfolk County Virginia Antiquary.

17 October 1791. John WATERMAN and Molly McCoy, orphan of William McCoy. Sur. Mason Hodges. John makes oath Molly is of lawful age.

21 March 1787. George WATKINS and Sarah Hacker. John Goforth, surety, makes oath that Sarah was born 4 April 1765. Married 22 March 1787 by Rev. Walker Maury.

3 January 1784. Robert WATKINS and Mrs. Elizabeth Jefferys. Sur. William Iagitts.

20 October 1759. Paul WATLINGTON and Jane Bickerdick. Sur. Richard Bickardick.

2 December 1787. Paul WATLINGTON and Elisabeth Beekly. Sur. Frances Beekley.

23 February 1792. Paul WATLINGTON and Mary Butler. Sur. William Whitfield. Paul makes oath Mary is of lawful age.

7 October 1789. Edward WATSON and Ann Lee, orphan of Francis Lee. Sur. John Willoughby. Edward makes oath Ann is of lawful age.

7 May 1771. George WATSON and Ann Brucker. Sur. Thomas Pearson.

30 August 1792. James WATSON and Mrs. Annis Watson. Sur. Jonathan Garrison.

12 September 1775. John WATSON and Jane Rogers. Ref: The Lower Norfolk County Virginia Antiquary.

5 January 1787. Major WATSON and Anniss Meloney. Sur. George Meloney.

17 August 1765. Hugh WATTS and Margaret Williamson. Sur. Joshua Williamson.

29 September 1787. James WEAR and Joice Webb. Nicholas Boosa or Boorz, makes oath that Joice is of lawful age and he is surety.

18 October 1759. George WEBB and Frances Ashley. Sur. Matthew Godfrey.

7 December 1769. George WEBB and Peggy Cheshire. Sur. Will Ballard.

24 June 1789. George WEBB and Catherine Veale. Sur. Thomas Veale, Sr. Married 25 June 1789 by Rev. Arthur Emmerson.

19 April 1744. James WEBB and Penelope Butt. Sur. Solomon Butt.

24 December 1767. James WEBB and Mrs. Alphia Langley. Sur. William Bradley.

9 November 1779. James WEBB, Jr. and Mrs. Sarah Shields. Sur. Willis Langley.

5 February 1779. John WEBB and Mrs. Elisabeth Keeton. Sur. John Whittham.

28 November 1792. Richard WEBB and Sally Bressie. Sur. Thomas Bressie, Jr.

18 December 1792. William WEBB and Sally Bailey. Sur. James Williams.

6 November 1790. Thomas WEBBER and Mrs. Dolly Reynolds. Sur. John May. Married 19 November 1790 by Rev. Arthur Emmerson.

17 August 1753. Francis WELDON and Ruth Pantale. Sur. Thomas Morris.

12 September 1765. Henry WELLS and Elizabeth Case. Sur. James Murphree.

19 November 1773. Henry WELLS, Jr. and Mary Benn, dau. of James Benn of Nansemond County, who consents for her. Sur. John Lee. Wit. George Benn and Mourning Benn.

17 March 1785. William WELLS and Nancy Curry. James Leitch, guardian of Nancy, consents for her and is surety.

26 October 1788. Thomas WEST and Margaret Willoughby. Married by Rev. Arthur Emmerson.

16 September 1782. Samuel WESTCOTT and Rody Eastwood. Sur. Elisha Eastwood.

3 August 1782. William WESTERHOUSE and Melia Simmons. Sur. Arthur Cooper.

22 May 1729. John WHIDDON and Mrs. Abigale Cawson. Sur. Christopher Cawson.

14 February 1758. John WHIDDON and Mary Corprew, dau. of Joshua Corprew, who consents for her. Sur. Alexander Bruce. Wit. Mary Loyall and Jane Baker.

22 September 1772. John WHIDDON, Jr. and Ann Herbert. Sur. John Herbert. John is the son of John Whiddon, Sr., who consents for him. Ann is the dau. of John Herbert. Wit. William Sisson and Mary Sisson.

16 December 1791. William WHITBY and Polly Reynolds. Sur. David Reynolds. William makes oath he is of lawful age. Married 17 December by Rev. Arthur Emmerson.

18 January 1787. John WHITE and Sally McDorman. Sur. Casper Herriter.

15 April 1760. Joshua WHITE and Lydia White, dau. of Patrick White, who consents for her. Sur. James Smith. Wit. Frances Clarke and Keader White.

30 August 1764. Samuel WHITE and Bithiah Bird. Sur. James Bird.

9 November 1787. William WHITE and Dinah Langley. Married by Rev. Walker Maury, who states William is of Richmond.

20 December 1782. John WHITEHEAD, Jr. and Ann Corprew. Sur. George D. Corprew.

21 January 1779. Edward WHITEHOUSE and Mary Lasher. Sur. John Hollowell.

27 March 1790. Charles WHITEHURST and Kezia Ventris. Sur. George Ventris. Charles makes oath he is of lawful age.

5 January 1779. Enoch WHITEHURST and Chloe Holstead, dau. of James Holstead, who consents for her. Sur. Robert Burley. Wit. Isaac Davis and Joseph Holstead.

14 June 1784. Richard WHITEHURST and Monica Nash. Surety not named. Thomas Nash, Jr. makes oath that Monica is of lawful age; no relationship stated.

10 January 1792. Ephraim WHITEMORE and Mrs. Sarah Nestor. Sur. Christopher Coffin.

20 November 1789. George WHITFIELD and Elisabeth Kinley. Sur. George Porter. Married 20 November 1789 by Rev. Arthur Emmerson.

10 December 1790. Francis WHITNEY and Elizabeth Woodside. Sur. John Woodside.

6 January 1783. Spiva WIATT and Elizabeth Lewelling. Sur. John Talbott. Note: Bond written Spiva Wiatt, signature Spievy Wyatt.

23 December 1789. Simon WILBON and Elizabeth Writin. William Williams, surety, makes oath that Elizabeth is the orphan of Thomas Writing and dau. of Elizabeth Writin.

16 January 1787. Lancaster WILBOURN and Margaret Cole. Sur. Henry Coal.

17 July 1792. Simon WILDBOAR and Fanny Issium, orphan of George Issium. Sur. George Thineball. Simon makes oath Fanny is of lawful age.

24 December 1782. James WILKENS and Mary Grimes. Sur. William Wilkins.

13 September 1764. Charles WILKINS and Mary Thompson. Sur. Thomas Newton.

13 August 1789. Ivey WILKINS and Mrs. Polly Ferebee. Sur. Robert Deford.

26 February 1791. James WILKINS and Mary Creekmur, dau. of Peter Creekmur, who consents for her and is surety. Wit. John Hall and John P. Sargeant.

14 September 1792. John WILKINS and Betsy Creekmur, dau. of Nicholas Creekmur, who consents for her. Sur. Jesse Grimes. Wit. Will. Creekmur. Note: Consent is addressed to Capt. William Wilson Clk.

22 April 1762. Joshua WILKINS and Lydia Northern, dau. of Philip Northern, who consents for her. Sur. Henry Wilson. Wit. Drury Sims and William Simmons.

6 January 1792. Robert WILKINS and Ann Stratton, orphan of Nathaniel Stratton. John Stratton, surety, makes oath Ann is of lawful age.

16 June 1766. William WILKINS and Tamer Burges. Sur. George Wright Burges.

30 December 1790. Willis WILKINS and Suckey Cherry. Married by Rev. Arthur Emmerson.

4 December 1790. Nicholas WILKINSON and Elizabeth Lewelling. Sur. John Trimble.

18 March 1789. John WILLEY and Nancy Waller. Sur. Paul Proby.

6 August 1790. Charles WILLIAMS and Martha Lewelling. Sur. Charles Williams.

23 December 1791. Daniel WILLIAMS and Bethiah Creekmur, dau. of Malachi Creekmur. Matthew Creekmur, surety, makes oath Bethiah is of lawful age. Daniel also makes oath he is of lawful age.

5 August 1790. Hollowell WILLIAMS and Mary Pool. Sur. Samuel Pool. Married 5 August 1790 by Rev. Arthur Emmerson.

21 December 1754. John WILLIAMS and Courtney Thelaball or Phillips. Sur. Philip Dison.

14 July 1779. John WILLIAMS and Hannah Warren, dau. of Mary Warren, who consents for her and states she is aged 21 years and 7 months. Sur. William Warren. Wit. Elizabeth Warren.

30 November 1782. John WILLIAMS and Peggy Jones. Sur. James Jones. David Kilgour, guardian of Peggy, consents for her.

28 May 1790. John WILLIAMS and Ann Nicholson. Sur. William Nicholson.

3 September 1787. Joseph WILLIAMS and Mrs. Ann Strong. Sur. John Williams.

25 August 1784. Lemuel WILLIAMS and Lydia Ferrebie. Emanuel Satchwell makes oath Lydia is of lawful age and is surety.

24 March 1785. Robert WILLIAMS and Anne Waters. Sur. John Williams.

20 May 1790. Robert WILLIAMS and Mrs. Mary Warren. Sur. John Williams.

29 November 1785. William WILLIAMS and Elisa' Harvy. Sur. Alexander Harvy.

1 May 1790. William WILLIAMS and Elisabeth Garriss. Sur. John Garriss. William makes oath he is of lawful age.

2 May 1792. William WILLIAMS and Leah Watlington, dau. of Elizabeth Watlington, who consents for her and makes oath she is of lawful age. Sur. Henry Sharp.

21 May 1791. Wilson WILLIAMS and Mary Avery. Sur. James Williams. Married 21 May by Rev. Arthur Emmerson.

18 September 1758. Francis WILLIAMSON and Martha Mathias. Sur. John Williamson.

25 July 1761. Francis WILLIAMSON and Kezia Mathias. Sur. Henry Jameson.

18 August 1774. James WILLIAMSON and Eliza Denby. Sur. Arthur Denby.

27 October 1785. James WILLIAMSON and Sarah Dunn. Sur. Nathaniel Murphy.

1 April 1755. John WILLIAMSON, Jr. and Mrs. Marv Mathias. Sur. John Williamson, Sr.

3 January 1760. John WILLIAMSON and Prudence Wilson. Sur. Samuel Boush.

9 September 1771. Joshua WILLIAMSON and Susanah Biddle. Sur. Robert Williamson. Wit. James Dunn. Note: At bottom of bond is written, "Sam Boush for Robt. Wmson, signing."

20 November 1766. Thomas WILLIAMSON and Margaret Wilson. Sur. John Williamson.

3 December 1768. Thomas WILLIAMSON and Mary Talbutt, dau. of William Talbot, who consents for her. Sur. John Williamson and John Ashley.

17 April 1790. William WILLIAMSON and Mary Singleton. Sur. John Singleton.

17 June 1779. Captain John WILLIS and Mary Dunn. Sur. Samuel Tomlinson. Samuel Davis makes oath that Mary is the dau. of John Dunn, deceased. Wit. Sally Brown and Caty Conyers.

21 February 1789. Walter WILLIS and Fanny Cann. James Cann, surety, makes oath that Fanny is the orphan of John Cann and is of lawful age. Married 24 February 1789 by Rev. Arthur Emmerson.

8 March 1787. Thomas WILLOCK and Elisabeth Farrer. Sur. William Farrier. Married 9 March 1787 by Rev. Walker Maury.

26 December 1743. John WILLOUGHBY and Mary Hutchings. Sur. Lemuel Willoughby.

21 April 1756. Major John WILLOUGHBY and Sarah Abyvon. Sur. George Abyvon.

18 September 1751. Lemuel WILLOUGHBY and Martha Sweny. Sur. William Ivy.

23 June 1791. Lemuel WILLOUGHBY and Elizabeth Wells. Sur. Henry Wells.

5 November 1779. Samuel WILLOUGHBY and Molly Marnex. Sur. Thomas Willoughby. Jemima Marnex, mother of Molly, makes oath Molly was born 6 April 1758 and consents for her. Wit. William Calvert.

11 December 1755. Thomas WILLOUGHBY and Mary Portlock. Sur. Lemuel Willoughby.

20 November 1783. William WILLOUGHBY and Margaret Marnex. Sur. Samuel Willoughby. Jemima Marnex, mother of Margaret, makes oath she is of lawful age.

24 January 1764. John WILLS and Mrs. Ann Childers. Sur. William Sisson.

7 December 1785. Benjamin WILSON and Elisabeth Parker. Sur. John Walker.

? ? 1738. Caleb WILSON and Mrs. Ann Church. Sur. Willis Wilson, Jr. Ref: The Lower Norfolk County Virginia Antiquary.

27 August 1787. Ephriam WILSON and Mary Morgain, dau. of Benjamin Morgan, who consents for her and states she was born 7 October 1764. Sur. Hunley Pead.

16 March 1772. George WILSON Jr. and Mary Faulkner. Charles Cooper surety, makes oath that Mary is the orphan of Thomas and Ann Faulkner, deceased.

20 July 1724. James WILSON, Sr. and Grace Phillips. Sur. Willis Wilson. Wit. Solomon Wilson.

20 August 1725. James WILSON and Dinah Nickason (Nicholson). Sur. Solomon Wilson. Wit. John Smith and Willis Wilson, Jr.

16 December 1743. James WILSON, Jr. and Grace Duke. Willis Wilson, brother of James, makes oath that Grace is almost 22 years of age. Wit. John Willoughby, J. Osheal and Samuel Boush, Jr.

10 August 1770. James WILSON and Mary Wilson. Sur. Colonel Josiah Wilson.

21 May 1746. Jermiah WILSON and Jane Wilson. Sur. James Butt. Note: Written on the bond is the statement that Jane is of age.

29 December 1760. John WILSON and Mary Happer. Sur. Samuel Happer.

17 September 1772. John WILSON, Gent. and Margaret Bruce. Ref: The Lower Norfolk County Virginia Antiquary.

2 August 1784. John WILSON and Mary Wormington, dau. of Abram Wormington, who consents for her. Sur. William Wilson yt. (youngest).

4 December 1771. Josiah WILSON and Margaret Cawson, dau. of Christopher and Margaret Cawson. Sur. Goodrich Boush. Note: It is stated that Josiah is the son of Colonel Josiah Wilson. Ref: The Lower Norfolk County Virginia Antiquary.

26 December 1785. Matthew WILSON and Nelly Kirby. Sur. Thomas Bonner.

16 August 1792. Simon WILSON and Sarah Warden. Sur. Nicholas Slack.

11 December 1752. Thomas WILSON and Prudence Nicholson. Sur. George Chamberlaine.

12 April 1791. Thomas WILSON and Nancy Happer. John Smith, yr., surety, makes oath Nancy is of lawful age. Thomas makes oath he, the son of Malachi Wilson, is of lawful age.

15 December 1792. Thomas WILSON and Elizabeth Hardy, orphan of James Hardy. William Tart, surety, makes oath Elizabeth is of lawful age.

11 December 1771. Captain William WILSON and Ann Butt. Sur. Malachi Wilson. William is son of Simon Wilson. Both William and Ann are of St. Brides Parish. Ref: The Lower Norfolk County Virginia Antiquary.

21 May 1789. William WILSON, Sr. and Sally Oliver. Malachi Miller, surety, makes oath that Sally is of lawful age.

7 June 1728. Willis WILSON and Eliza' Goodrich. Sur. Solomon Wilson. Wit. John Smith.

4 August 1787. Henry Wilstock and Catherine Flinn. Married by Rev. Walker Maury.

10 January 1763. Samuel WISE and Mary Blackburn. Sur. Samuel Boush. Rev. Charles Smith makes oath that Mary, the dau. of Margaret McNeil and John Blackburn, was born in 1742.

2 May 1778. Thomas WISHART and Juliet White. Sur. Matthew Godfrey.

3 January 1792. William WONYCUTT and Margaret Jenkins, orphan of James Jenkins. Sur. Nicholas Wonycutt. William Wonycutt makes oath Margaret is of lawful age.

22 September 1712. Charles WOOD and Mary Katherine. Sur. Hugh Danill. Note: Name of bride appears to be incomplete.

10 March 1787. David WOOD and Nancy Cuthrell, dau. of Eliza' Cuthrell, who consents for her. Sur. Thomas Evins.

20 May 1787. Godfrey WOOD and Barbara Cooper, dau. of Charles Cooper, who consents for her. Sur. Robert Woodside. Wit. Charles Cooper, Jr.

7 November 1792. Joshua WOOD and Susanna Kay. Sur. Thomas Crafts.

28 November 1787. Nicholas WOODARD and Mrs. Elizabeth Holstead. Sur. Matthew Creekmur.

3 January 1785. Thomas WOODARD and Mrs. Argent Randolph. Sur. David Fentress.

2 October 1790. Joshua WOODHOUSE and Sally Peede. Sur. Joshua Peed. Joshua makes oath he is of lawful age.

31 May 1760. John WOODSID(E) and Jane Bird. Sur. James Bird.

2 February 1760. Abraham WORMINGTON and Mary Portlock. Sur. Thomas Jones. Note: Bond written Abraham; signature Abram.

24 July 1784. William WORMINGTON and Mary Silvester. Sur. John Wilson. Daniel Sanford makes oath William and Mary are of lawful age.

19 October 1785. George WOTTEN and Mrs. Mary Neglee. Sur. John Sclater.

12 September 1753. Christopher WRIGHT and Mary Walke. Sur. Anthony Walke.

1 June 1770. Francis WRIGHT and Ann Godfrey Tatem. Sur. John Tatem.

16 January 1769. Joshua WRIGHT and Lucretia Fry, dau. of Robert Fry, who consents and makes oath she is 26 years of age. Sur. Samuel Boush.

16 September 1779. Miles WRIGHT and Mrs. Elisabeth Deans. Sur. Samuel Veale.

12 August 1778. Captain Patrick WRIGHT and Lucy Kelly, sister of George Kelly. Sur. John Fowler. Ref: The Lower Norfolk County Virginia Antiquary.

13 August 1724. Stephen WRIGHT and Katherine (?) Jossey (?) (illegible). Sur. Solomon Wilson. Wit. Anthony Walke, and John Smith.

19 March 1761. Stephen WRIGHT and Ann Phripp. Sur. John Phripp.

9 March 1792. Thomas WRIGHT and Mrs. Orpy Taylor. Sur. John Bruce.

15 February 1745. William WRIGHT and Mary Butt. Sur. Charles Smith.

30 October 1793. William WRIGHT and Mrs. Molly Thompson. Sur. George Peed.

9 June 1784. Millerson WRIGHTON and Elizabeth Wildair, dau. of Edward Wilder, who consents for her. Sur. Joshua Peaton. Wit. Josua Milison and James Lambert. Note: Written Millerson Wrighton in Bond, signature Millison Riten or Biten. Wildair in Bond, signature of Edward is Wilder.

24 December 1789. Joshua WYATT and Anne Ives. Sur. Robert Ives. Note: Written on Bond is the statement that Anne's guardian consented (however, guardian not named).

24 April 1791. William YEATES and Mrs. Patience Hogwood. Sur. James Wright. Married 2 May by Rev. Arthur Emmerson.

20 May 1784. James YOUNG and Mrs. Sarah Purviance. Sur. Robert Elliot.

INDEX

A

Abyvon,
  Sarah 73
Addison,
  Susannah 15
Airs,
  Frances 40
Aitchison,
  Ann 35
Alexander,
  Sarah 27
Alwincle-Alwinkle,
  Catherine 2
  Susannah 7
Andrews,
  Leah 28
Anguish,
  Mary 1
Archer,
  Mary 1
  Rebecca 64
  Susannah 59
Arnott,
  Elizabeth 20
  Mary 58
Ashley,
  Elizabeth 39
  Frances 69
  Lydia 14
  Mary 7,16
  Molley 4
Avary-Avery,
  Ann 26
  Elizabeth 46
  Margaret 23
  Mary 44,72
  Nancy 28

B

Bacon,
  Elizabeth 64
  Lydia 23
  Rebecca 6
Bailey,
  Ann 65
  Edith 19
  Frances 25
  Mary 9,12
  Sally 69
  Susannah 32
Baker,
  ---cca (Rebecca?) 39
Balentine-Ballentine,
  Abi 51
  Agness 29
  Ann 32,43
  Elizabeth 46
  Frances 59
  Jamima 2
Ball,
  Kezia 39
Ballance,
  Abigail 17
  Mary 17
Ballard,
  Ann 54
  Catherine 6
  Eliza 1
Banks,
  Mary 54
Barlow,
  Ann 12
Barnes,
  Ollife 26
Barocherfour,
  Anna Maria 42

Barr,
  Sealey 62
Barraud,
  Sarah 64
Barringer,
  Mary 43
Barrington,
  Hannah 43
Bartee,
  Eliza 11
  Frances 3,59
  Mary 31
  Peggy 39
Bascome,
  Lydia 6
  Molly 47
Bashaw,
  Molly 30
Bass,
  Elizabeth 28
Batchelor,
  Sarah 19
Bayne,
  Ann 44
  Elizabeth 56
  Sarah 27
Beckley,
  Judy 64
Beekly,
  Elisabeth 69
Beetley,
  Nanny 38
Belgrove,
  Dinah 1
Bell,
  Margaret 8,48
  Susanna 8
Benn,
  Ann 59
  Mary 69
Bentel,
  Lovey 59
Benthall,
  Betsy 51
Besan,
  Dinah 43
Best,
  ----- 9
  Charity 55
Bevan,
  Dinah (See Besan) 43
  Mary 53
Bickerdick,
  Jane 68
Biddle,
  Susanah 72
Bingham,
  Rachael 40
Bird,
  Betsey 46
  Bithiah 70
  Jane 75
Blackburn,
  Mary 75
Blades,
  Rebecca 68
Blake,
  Elisabeth 29
  Elizabeth 37
Bland,
  Ann 15
Boulton,
  Lydia 9
Boush,
  Catherine 49
  Eliza 15
  Elizabeth 66
  Margaret 54

Boush, (cont'd)
  Mary 11
  Peggy 11
Boushell,
  Ann 11
  Nancy 4
  Susannah 37
Boyd,
  Margaret 35
  Teresa 51
Boyles,
  Sarah 37
Bradley,
  Betsy 8
Braithwait,
  Lucretia 1
Bramble,
  Elizabeth 20
Brannon,
  Ann 51
Brazill,
  Jane 40
Breadey,
  Mary 62
Bressie,
  Sally 69
Brett,
  Eliza 35
  Elizabeth 47
  Frances 2
Brian,
  Elizabeth 47
Brickell,
  Celia 63
Bridger,
  Mary 38
Brodie,
  Martha 38
  Sarah 45
Brough,
  Sarah 44
Brown,
  Anna 13
  Catherine 51
  Elisabeth 51
  Jane 13
  Margaret 12
  Mary 59,60
  Nancy 61
Browning,
  Elizabeth 30,55
Bruce,
  Elizabeth 5,27
  Margaret 74
  Susanna 39
Brucker,
  Ann 69
Bryan,
  Ann 44
  Mary 51
Buckley,
  Betty 30
Bully,
  Sarah 66
Bunting,
  Fanny 5
  Lydia 8
Burdess,
  Mary 63
Burges-Burgess,
  Betsy 24
  Mary 10,31,68
  Tamer 22,71
Burnet-Burnett,
  Elizabeth 3
  Mary 7
Burns,
  Judy 32

Burton,
  Mary 33
But----,
  Nancy 65
Butler,
  Mary 69
  Sarah 62
Butt,
  Ann 53,74
  Courtney 34
  Dina(h) 11
  Edith 37
  Elizabeth 40
  Jemima 13
  Kez-- 10
  Mary 10,30,47,53,76
  Peggy 57
  Penelope 69
  Sarah 4,8,26,39,47

C

Callis,
  Sarah 15
Calvert,
  Elizabeth 41
  Frances 56
  Hellen 43
  Lucy 54
  Mary 2,40,67
  Polly 43
Camack,
  Sarah 18
Campbell,
  Frances 26
  Isabella 41
Cann,
  Fanny 73
  Sarah 7,62
Carbery,
  Sarah 41
Carney,
  Ann 35
  Charity 33
  Elizabeth Wright 63
  Mary 14
  Nancy 30
  Sarah 64
  Westcoat 14
Carrol,
  Elizabeth 26
Carter,
  Elizabeth 41
  Joice 21
  Mary 13,52
Cartwright,
  Mary 18
Case,
  Elizabeth 69
  Frances 44
Cawson,
  Abigail 29,48
  Abigale 70
  Ann 3
  Janet 32
  Kezia 53
  Lydia 49
  Margaret 74
Chandler,
  Mary 51
Cherry,
  Frances 58
  Mary 45
  Polly 13
  Suckey 71
  Tamer 16
Cheshire,
  Peggy 69
Childers,
  Ann 73
  Frances 68

Childers, (cont'd)
  Sarah 27
Church,
  Abiah 62
  Ann 73
  Julian 62
  Sarah 56
Clarkson,
  Mary 9
Cleeves,
  Ann 61
  Elizabeth 66
Coffield,
  Elizabeth 56
Cole,
  Margaret 71
  Mary 66
Collart,
  Mary 3
Colley,
  Dinah 19
  Elizabeth 18
  Lydia 28
Connelly,
  Mary 15
Conner,
  Abigail 54
  Elizabeth 66
  Margaret 15
  Mary 21,36
Connor,
  Margaret 4
  Sukey 15
Consaul,
  Mary 3
Conyers,
  Ann 57
  Nancy 48
Cooke,
  Lucy 55
Cooper,
  Barbara 75
  Elisabeth 54
  Fanny 17
  Mary 20,23,68
  Rhoda 68
  Rosanna 32
  Sarah 33,41,45
  Thamer 67
Corprew,
  Ann 70
  Ellenor 4
  Eupan 60
  Mary 70
  Sarah 59
Cotton,
  Elizabeth 50
Coverley-Coverly,
  Ann 34
  Elizabeth 43
Cowper,
  Hannah 62
Cratchet,
  Nancy 47
Creech,
  Elisabeth 53
  Elizabeth 39
Creekmur,
  Bethiah 71
  Betsy 71
  Cloe 45
  Mary 71
  Tamar 33
Crofts,
  Elizabeth 13
Culpeper-Culpepper,
  Agness 17
  Ann 13
  Frankey 55
  Hannah 20
  Margaret 56,66
  Peggy 18
  Sarah 34

Curle,
  Elizabeth 9
Curry,
  Nancy 70
Cuthrell,
  Nancy 75

D

Dale,
  Ann 15,60
  Dinah 15
  Elizabeth 32,37,42
  Hannah 11
  Margaret 28
  Mary Ann 2
  Prudence 58
  Sarah 14
Dameron,
  Fanny 67
  Winea 16
Darby,
  Mary 25
  Susannah 45
Darley,
  Mary (See Darby) 25
Davidson,
  Martha 50
Davis,
  Ann 24
  Elisabeth 48
  Ellen Whittle 22
  Jane 15
  Patience 68
Day,
  Frances 8
Deal-Deale,
  Lydia 14
  Margaret 22
  Mary 43
Deans,
  Elisabeth 45,75
  Nancy 18
  Sarah 33
Delson,
  Anne (See Dolson) 24
Denby,
  Elisabeth 36
  Eliza 72
  Elizabeth 43
  Mary 38,48
  Sarah 3,67
  Susanna 21
Deveo,
  Sarah 2
Dial,
  Elizabeth 50
Dickenson,
  Elizabeth 68
Dickson,
  Judith 23
  Sabra 8
Dison,
  Charity 1
  Jane 10
  Sarah 32,60
Doe,
  Elizabeth (See Dale) 42
Dogget,
  Nancy 16
Dolson,
  Anne 24
Donnell,
  Ann 9
Dorvey,
  Christian 6
Doudge,
  Frances 42
Dougle,
  Mary 5
Doyle,
  Mary 20

Drewry,
  Sarah 44
  Venus 67
Drummond,
  Jane 41
Drury,
  Mary 22,24
  Sarah 62
Duche,
  Hannah 38
Dudley,
  Ann 60
  Mary 20
Duff,
  Mary 67
Duffie,
  Margaret 31
Duke,
  Grace 74
Dunderwin,
  Dicay 4
Dunn,
  Ann 30,41
  Elizabeth 10,57
  Mary 73
  Sarah 12,67,72
Dupree,
  Sarah 1

                E

Easter,
  Mary 65
Eastwood,
  Charlotte 12
  Elizabeth 67
  Mary 54,64
  Nancy 51
  Phebe 64
  Rody 70
Eauner,
  Margaret 47
Eddenton,
  Mary 57
Edmonds,
  Courtnay 54
Edmunds,
  Catherine 8
Edwards,
  Bathia(h) 66
  Dinah 18
  Joyce 50
  Mary Ann 1,15
  Mary 21
  Sophia 31,48
Ellegood,
  Fernelia 36
Elliott,
  Margaret 37
  Rose 50
Ellis,
  Ann 23
  Elizabeth 18
  Frances 6
  Kezia 64
  Sarah 45
Ellison,
  Mary 44
Emberson,
  Elizabeth 55
Esther,
  Susannah 13
Etheredge-Etheridge,
  Barthiah 59
  Elisabeth 42,62
  Margaret 19,27
  Mary 4,22,23,37,45
  Molly 32
  Sarah 44
Eustace,
  Catherine 5

Everage,
  Sarah 13
Evington,
  Molly 20
Ewel-Ewell,
  Mary 7,33
Eyre,
  Margaret 40

                F

Fairfield,
  Elizabeth 10
Falioner,
  Eliza 4
Farr,
  Alby 67
Farrer,
  Elisabeth 73
Faulkner,
  Mary 73
Fells,
  Polly 58
Ferbee,
  Ann 37
Ferrebie-Ferebee,
  Lydia 72
  Mary 3
  Polly 71
Ferrol,
  Ann 10
Fife,
  Elizabeth 51
  Mary 56
Fisher,
  Druscilla 21
Flinn,
  Catherine 74
Footit,
  Mary 19
  Sally 29
Foreman,
  Courtney 33
  Lovey 18
  Lydia 24
  Mary 60
Franks,
  Ann 63
  Elizabeth 13
  Isabel 65
Frazier,
  Frances 54
Fredlee,
  Mary 33
Freeman,
  Frances 44
  Mary 10
  Patience 22
Fridley,
  Director 25
Frier,
  Mary 32
Frost,
  Margaret 37
Fry,
  Lucretia 75
  Mary 57
Furbee,
  Martha 36
Furlong,
  Mary 35
Furnace,
  Elizabeth 38

                G

Gale,
  Ann 55
Galt,
  Sarah 12

Gamewell,
  Sarah 4
Gardner,
  Elizabeth 2
  Mary 33
Garnes,
  Elizabeth 16
  Sarah 45
Garriss,
  Elisabeth 72
Garroway,
  Jemima 42
Gawthony,
  Jane 20
Gibson,
  Mary 55
Giles,
  Mary 46
  Philarity 34
Gilmour,
  Charlotte 9
Godfrey,
  Anne 42,67
  Elisabeth 68
  Eliza 2
  Elizabeth 46
  Katy 38
  Martha 37,38
  Mary 14,32,57
  Meriam 5
Godman,
  Olive 30
Godwin,
  Ann 65
Golt,
  Ann 31
Goodrich,
  Agatha Wells 58
  Elizabeth 74
  Molly 58
Goosburg,
  Elizabeth 10
Gordon,
  Ann 9
  Elisabeth 18
  Elizabeth 56
  Mary 15
Graham,
  Sally 45
Grant,
  Dinah 30
Gray,
  Elizabeth 25
  Nancy 18
Grear,
  Alice 62
Gregory,
  Elizabeth 60
Griffin,
  Christian 24
  Laetitia 27
Griggs,
  Mary 53
  Peggy 41
Grigory,
  Ann 26
Grimes,
  Anne 5
  Betsy 21
  Juley 33
  Louisa 37
  Lydia 34,67
  Mary 27,38,71
  Sarah 12,41,53
Gumbly,
  Ann 24
Guy,
  Bridget-Bridgett 20,65
  Nancy 9
Gwin-Gwynn,
  Elizabeth 58
  Mildred 37

H

Hacker,
  Sarah 68
Hainsworth,
  Molly 58
Haire,
  Nancy 67
Hall,
  Elizabeth 41
  Fanny 27
  Frances 11,31
  Martha 59
Hamilton,
  Mary 28
  Nancy 56
Hanaly,
  Susannah 1
Hanbury,
  Betty 60
Hancocke,
  Molly 21
Hansford,
  Elizabeth 26
  Mary 52
Hansly,
  Susannah (See Hanaly)1
Happer,
  Abigail 22
  Elizabeth 11
  Mary 29,74
  Nancy 74
Hardy,
  Elizabeth 74
Harmon-Harmmon,
  Rebecca 4
  Sally 39
Harper,
  Mary 4
Harris,
  Mary 13
Harrison,
  Ludwell 53
Hartfoot,
  Mary 61
Hartford,
  Catherine 53
Harvy-Harvey,
  Elizabeth 72
  Rebecca 58
Hatton,
  Elizabeth 21
Hawkins,
  Lydia 65
Heley,
  Mary 8
Hennicke,
  Katy 38
Herbert,
  Abigail 34
  Ann 42,70
  Elizabeth 21,48,56,63
  Fanny 10
  Janet 50
  Lydia 13,53
  Margaret 41
  Martha 19
  Mary 29,57
  Tabitha 41
Herriter,
  Mary 2
Hewit,
  Jemima 29
Higgins,
  Sally 51
  Susanna 16
Hiley,
  Elizabeth 22
  Flora 35
Hill,
  Judah 40
  Mary 53
  Molly 62

Hilman
  Judith 41
Hilton,
  Sarah 21
Hobbs,
  Sarah 5
Hodges-Hodgis,
  Ann 12
  Bathiah 17
  Disey 42
  Elizabeth 27
  Isabella 30
  Lois 27
  Lydia 7,49
  Mary 17,26,32,40
  Nancy 61
  Sarah 12
Hodgson,
  Elizabeth 45
Hoffler,
  Kezia 3
Hogwood,
  Patience 76
Holdness,
  Elizabeth 7
Holland,
  Susanna 43
Hollowell,
  Ann 46
Holstead,
  Betty Anne 17
  Chloe 70
  Elizabeth 75
  Mary (3) 10
  Sally 10
Holt,
  Elizabeth 39
  Mary 51
Hopkins,
  Rebecca 2
Horton,
  Elizabeth 31
Howard,
  Pattey 51
Hubbard,
  Ann 3
Hudson,
  Ann 6
  Eliza 2,7
  Mary 54
Hughes,
  Ann 45
  Jennet 59
  Margaret 52
  Mary 33
Hunter,
  Mary 61
Hutchings,
  Elizabeth 5
  Mary 55,73
Hutton,
  Margaret 56
Hyllard,
  Mourning 15

I

Ingham,
  Parnell 1
Inkson,
  Dinah 35
Insell,
  Mary 23
Irish,
  Polly 31
Ishon,
  Rosanna 16
Isorns,
  Jenny 41
Issium,
  Fanny 71

Ives,
  Anne 76
  Aphia 9
Ivy,
  Alif 46
  Ann 7
  Elizabeth 9,61,62
  Mary 35

J

Jack,
  Jennet 2
Jackson,
  Mary 39
  Sarah 2
Jacobs,
  Anne 25,26
  Rebecca 7
James,
  Mary 3
Jarvis,
  Prudence 44
  Sarah 43
Jasper,
  Susannah 44
Jeffries-Jefferys,
  Elizabeth 68
  Sarah 25
Jeffery,
  Mary 16
Jenings-Jennings,
  Ann 56
  Elizabeth 15
Jenkins,
  Esther 62
  Margaret 75
Jenning,
  Hester 45
Jim,
  Ann (See Join) 47
Jocey,
  Elizabeth 36
Joel,
  Rebecca 3
Johnson,
  Cosiah 35
  Judith 2
  Mary 56
Johnston,
  Elizabeth 60
Join,
  Ann 47
Jolliff-Jolliffe,
  Celia 54
  Elizabeth 60
  Sarah 11
  Susanna 24
Jones,
  Clotilda 39
  Elizabeth 1
  Frances 15
  Keziah 67
  Martha 15
  Mary 4,28
  Peggy 72
  Sarah 24,25
Josey,
  Anne 35
  Mary 36
Jossey, (?)
  Katherine (?) 75

K

Katherine,
  Mary 75
Kay,
  Franky 62
  Susanna 75

Keaton-Keeton,
 Elisabeth 69
 Mary 23
 ----- 19
Kellum,
 Comfort 68
Kelly,
 Lucy 75
Kelsick,
 Anne 36
 Eleanora 47
 Isabella 26
Kelso,
 Elizabeth 5
Ker,
 Frances 30
Ketor,
 Cortney 9
Kidd,
 Ann 29
Kinder,
 Charity 16
King,
 Ann 16
Kingston,
 Margaret 62
Kinley,
 Elisabeth 71
Kinner,
 Sarah 14
 Sophia 65
Kirby,
 Nelly 74
Kirkley,
 Isabella 36
Kite,
 Ann 61
Knight,
 Anne 50

L

Lakeland,
 Martha 55
Lamb,
 Sarah 62
Lambert,
 Elisabeth 28
 Tamer 32
Lamount,
 Elisabeth 29
 Elizabeth 52
 Leah 25
Lancaster,
 Sarah 60
Langley,
 Alphia 69
 Dinah 70
 Eliza 2
 Elizabeth 20,47,63
 Frances 5
 Leticy 51
 Margaret 30
 Mary 9
 Sarah 51
Larchen,
 Elizabeth 40
Lasher,
 Mary 70
Latham,
 Polly 45
Lee,
 Ann 69
 Sarah 34
Leitch,
 Elizabeth 23
Lewling,
 Dinah 35
Lewelling,
 Ann-Anne 15,21
 Elizabeth 39,(2),71

Lewelling, cont'd.
 Frances 36
 Letta 9
 Lydia 35
 Margaret 21
 Martha 48,71
 Sally 12
Lockhart,
 Sarah 38
Logan,
 Susanna 20
Lovett-Lovitt
 Elizabeth 23
 Mary 23
Lowe,
 Amy 3
Lowery-Lowrey,
 Courtney 13
 Elizabeth 28
 Frances 35
 Mary 36
 Tabitha 49
Loyall,
 Susanna 3
Luke,
 Elizabeth 53
Lush,
 Ann 7
 Rhoda 26

Mc

McClean,
 Nancy 28
McClenahan,
 Mary 45
McCloud,
 Ann 32
 Fanny (2) 61
 Honour 14
McCoy,
 Dinah 42
 Elizabeth 22
 Margaret 57
 Mary Ann 40
 Molly 68
 Penelope 11
McCurdy,
 Elizabeth 45
McDonald,
 Susannah 13
McDorman,
 Sally 70
McDowell,
 Mary 61
McDurman,
 Margaret 7
McGee,
 Catherine 10
McGuire,
 Margaret 10
McHenry,
 Peggy 15
McKay,
 Rachael 17
McLachlan-McLacklan,
 Director 25
 Jane 52
McNary,
 Mary 2
McPherson,
 Elisabeth 17
 Fanny 66
 Sally 58
Mcrea,
 Selah Cherry 54
 (See Marcer)

M

Mackie,
 Mary 47
Macneil,
 Mary 53
Madden,
 Margaret 7
Mahanes,
 Catharine 67
Makins,
 Nancy 8
Malbone,
 Apphia 29
Maning-Manning,
 Ann 19
 Isabella 49
 Margaret 30
 Martha 50
 Mary 30
 Phebe 31
 Sarah 3,36,62
Mansfield,
 Barbara 46
 Lydia 25
 Mary 50
Marley,
 Elizabeth 46
Marcer,
 Selah Cherry 54
Marnex,
 Margaret 73
 Molly 73
Marshall,
 Mary 57
Mason,
 Abigail 22
 Frances 52
 Peggy 4
Mather,
 Ann 36
Mathers,
 Catharine 57
Mathias-Matthias,
 ----- 49
 Ann 34
 Katy 48
 Kezia 72
 Martha 72
 Mary 72
 Rebecca 19
Maund,
 Elisabeth 62
 Elizabeth 3
 Martha 58
 Prudence 35
Mayle,
 A-ne 30
 Margaret 27
Meloney,
 Anniss 69
Mercer,
 Rachel 50
Mesler,
 Elizabeth 33
Miars,
 Mary 28
 Sarah 23
Milburn,
 Susannah 39
Miles,
 Jane 31
Miller,
 Catherin 59
 Dinah 14
 Elizabeth 40
 Lydia 24,34
 Mary 11,14,43,47
 Patty 22
 Polly 68
 Sarah 60

Millison,
Ann	34
Lydia	32

Millow,
Peggy	30

Milner,
Priscilla	60

Minner,
Amelia	14

Mitchel-Mitchell,
Elienor	48
Sarah	19

Mohun,
Margaret	43

Moody,
Elizabeth	21

Moore,
Catherine	33
Courtney	17,58
Elisabeth	14
Elizabeth	4
Isabella	12
Lydia	13
Margaret	59
Mary	14,46

Morgain-Morgan,
Mary	66,73
Rhodah	8

Morisson,
Mary	61

Morris,
Lucy	4
Mary	23
Nancey	25
Sally	17

Moseley-Mosely,
Blandinah	7
Edith	47
Martha	27
Mary	11

Mott,
Juda	8

Moye,
White	49

Mumford,
Frances Moseley	6

Munro,
Barbara	6

Murden,
Mary	23,37
Max (?)	10
Sarah	7

Murdock,
Mary	1

Murray,
Elizabeth	38
Sarah	41

Murrow,
Grace	19

Mushrow,
Polly	28

N

Nash,
Dinah	63
Elizabeth	35,53
Frances Ann	21
Lydia	43
Mary	6
Monica	70

Neglee,
Mary	75

Nelson,
Elizabeth	46

Nestor,
Sarah	70

Newton,
Ann	33
Elizabeth	11
Rebecca	47

Nichols-Nicols,
Drusilla	55
Elizabeth	12

Nicholas,
Elizabeth	27

Nicholson,
Ann	31,55,72
Lydia	51
Mary	34
Prudence	74

Nickason (Nicholson),
Dinah	74

Nickhalson,
Sarah	39

Niol,
Mary	19

Norcut,
Judith	57

Northcott,
Sarah	34

Northern,
Lydia	71

Nosay,
Anne	40

Noyall,
Mary	19

O

Oagely,
Elizabeth	64

Odean-Odeon,
Frances	46
Mary	48

Oliver,
Sally	74

Orange,
Mary	57

Osheal,
Ann	34
Elizabeth	59

Owens-Owins,
Ann	19
Elizabeth	52
Frances	18
Jennet	9
Mary	13
Priciller	9
Sally	57

P

Pades,
Lucretia	27

Palmer,
Mary	19

Pantale,
Ruth	69

Parke,
Mary	68

Parker,
Elisabeth	73
Mary	49

Parrish,
Peggy	5

Parsons,
Franky	59

Pasteur,
Mary	16

Pead-Peed-Peede,
Ann	33
Jacamine	28
Sally	27,75
Sarah	24

Pearce,
Ann	65

Pearson,
Nancy	42
Rebecca	57

Peaton-Peaton,
Ann	39
Keziah	17

Pedes,
Mary	37

Perkins,
Eda	42
Elisabeth	5

Peyton,
Mary	5
Sarah	23

Philips-Phillips-Phillipps,
Ann	46
Elizabeth	28
Grace	74
Mary	14
Nancy	46
Susanna	20

Phripp,
Ann	76
Hannah	63

Pilkington,
Mary	45

Pippin,
Mary	37

Playstead,
Mary	44

Pool-Poole,
Elizabeth	47
Mary	45,48,72
Sally	17
Sarah	4

Porter,
Abigail	26
Ann	38,43
Karen	16
Mary	29
Patience	49

Portlock,
Abiah	53
Ann	48
Elisabeth	52
Elizabeth	44
Keziah	36
Lydia	22
Mary	21,24,48,62,73,75
Peggy	20,31
Rebecca	58,63
Sarah	35

Powell,
Catherine	12
Peggy	54

Prata,
Courtney	39

Pratt,
Mary	27

Prescott,
Ann	3

Price,
Frances	13
Lydia	57

Pritchard,
Dolly	38
Mason	36,40

Proby,
Sophia	28

Pugh,
Mary	54

Pullen,
Mary	25

Pullet,
Mary	60

Pulling,
Nancy	65

Purviance,
Sarah	76

R

Ramsey,
  Ann 35
  Sarah 2
Randolph,
  Argent 75
Reade-Reed,
  Dorothy 37
  Peggy 19
Redd,
  Ann 65
  Elisabeth 20
  Joice 15
  Susanna 20
Reynolds,
  Dolly 69
  Polly 70
Rhonald,
  Mary 64
Richard,
  Louisa 64
Richards,
  Elizabeth 24
Richardson,
  Elizabeth 50,66
  Lydia 18
  Mary 42
Riddick,
  Elizabeth 53
Riddlehurst,
  Martha 10
Ritch,
  Margaret 64
Ritter,
  Cherry 1
  Polly 8
Rives,
  Margaret 42
Roach,
  Jemimah 52
Robe,
  Mary 28
Roberts,
  Courtney 16
  Elisabeth 51
Robins,
  Adah 38
Robinson,
  Frances 25
  Jane 46
  Mary 54
Rogers,
  Ann 40
  Jane 69
  Priscilla 42
Ross,
  Mary 65,68
  Peggy 11
Rosseter,
  Elizabeth 58
Rothery,
  Ann 57
  Elizabeth 25
  Mary 55
Rudder,
  Elizabeth 46
  Hannah 3
Russell,
  Patience 28
  Sarah 21
Rutter,
  Cherry 31
  Mary 31

S

Sanford,
  Sarah 43
Satchwell,
  Suckey 32

Saunders,
  Dianna 5
Savage,
  Mary 11
Savells,
  Abigail 51
  Peggy 32
Savills,
  Keziah 60
Sceady,
  Elizabeth 39
Scottk
  Dinah 47
  Margaret 15
  Martha 58
  Mary 30
  Nancy 32
  Prudence 65
Shafer,
  Mary 50
  Sally 18
Sharp,
  Mary 46
Sheald-Shields,
  Elizabeth 28
  Fanny 58
  Jenet 41
  Mary 49
  Sarah 69
Shepherd,
  Elizabeth 2
Shermedine,
  Elizabeth 51
Shipwash,
  Biar 4
  Courtney 23
  Martha 7
Shore,
  Ann 19,56
Short,
  Sarah 23
Sikes,
  Elisabeth 52
  Kezia 34
  Mary 53
Sills,
  Mary 54
Silverthorn,
  Susanna 36
Silvester,
  Ann 14
  Elizabeth 12
  Mary 75
  Sarah 36
Simmons,
  Elisabeth 38
  Mary 16
  Melia 70
Simpson,
  Ann 25
Singleton,
  Elizabeth 58
  Mary 73
  Sally 57
Sisson,
  Jane 44
Skinner,
  Ann 26
  Elizabeth 27
  Jane 66
Sparrow,
  Betty 31
  Dinah 66
  Elizabeth 64
  Frances 12
  Mary 21
  Peggy 31
  Sarah 45
Spencer,
  Elizabeth 28
Spooner,
  Eleanor 17

Slaughter,
  Mary 17
Smallwood,
  Nancy 1
Smith,
  Abey 63
  Alice 64
  Ann 65
  Celia 11
  Christian 24
  Edey 18
  Elisabeth 54,62
  Elizabeth 18,37
  Hannah 9
  Lydia 42
  Martha 14
  Mary 63
  Mary Ann 58
  Peggy 62
  Sarah 16,35
Smithson,
  Martha 36
  Mary 8
Snale,
  Ann 43
  Elizabeth 39
Somerville,
  Dorothy 52
Southerland,
  Elisabeth 21
Southerlin,
  Sarah 4
Stackpole,
  Rebecca 13
Stafford,
  Hannah 27
Stamers-Stammers,
  Dorrity 16
  Sarah 61
Standey,
  Elizabeth 57
Stanley,
  Mary 36
Stant,
  Sarah 59
Stark,
  Clavy 57
Starr,
  Katherine 48
Steel,
  Elizabeth 7
  Jane 2
  Sarah 2
Stewart,
  Eliza 60
  Elizabeth 67
  Faith 42
  Jemimah 29
  Lydia 58
  Mary 50
Stokes,
  Mary 23
Stratton,
  Ann 71
Streep,
  Margaret 3
Strong,
  Ann 72
Stroud,
  Anne 22,40
Sweny-Sweney,
  Ann 6
  Elizabeth 63
  Martha 6,73
  Uphan 14
Symonds,
  Sarah 3
Synott,
  Ann 37

T

Tabb,
Elizabeth 6
Mary 6,63
Talbot-Talbutt,
Ann 35
Diane 7
Elizabeth 5,63
Lockey 28
Mary 22,73
Penelope 60
Sarah 20,63
Suckie 44
Tart-Tarrt,
Livinia 50
Mary 8
Nancy 66
Tatem,
Ann 50,75
Diana 31
Lovet 49
Lydia 66
Mirium 22
Taylor,
Abigail 52
Ann 29
Frankey 50
Jenny 25
Latitia 6
Louisa 1
Margaret 6,23
Maron 68
Martha 61
Mary 2,5,25,50,63
Orpy 76
Sarah 41
Tennis,
Hannah 15
Terry,
Susanna 40
Thelaball,
Abigail 26
Courtney 72
Mary 22
Mary Ann 5
Sarah 47
Susanna 19
Thenabal,
Ann 32
Thomas,
Lydia 33
Thompson-Thomson,
Agnes 41
Ann 20
Margaret 48
Mary 17,71
Molly 76
Thruston,
Elizabeth 11
Tigner,
Ann 20
Timberlake,
Euphan 47
Tomer,
Frances 60
Tomough,
Martha 65
Tracey,
Mary 1
Tucker,
Caroline Henrietta 49
Courtney 6,67
Elizabeth 61
Frances 11,48
Joanna 16
Martha 49
Mary 31
Rebecca 14
Sarah 64
Tumblin,
Margaret 24

Tumer,
Elizabeth 45
Turner,
Ann 17

V

Valentine-Vallentine,
Anne 24
Frances 3
Veal-Veale,
Agnis 53
Catherine 50,69
Elizabeth 31
Margaret 12
Mary 14,26,56
Sally 12,27
Ventris,
Kezia 70
Volum-Volume,
Elisabeth 62
Hannah 59

W

Wadlington,
Elizabeth 54
Wakefield,
Elizabeth 26
Sarah 50
Walke,
Mary 75
Sally 8
Walker,
Ann 55
Elizabeth 47
Jane 12
Mary 7,8,33
Wall,
Jane 40
Wallace,
Joyce 2
Margaret 64
Polly 61
Waller,
Anne 57
Nancy 71
Wallis,
Martha 59
Walmsley,
Elizabeth 29
Ellender 36
Mary 16
Ward,
Diana 24
Margaret 37
Mary 64,68
Warden,
Mary 60
Sarah 74
Warner,
Elizabeth 47
Warren,
Hannah 72
Mary 72
Waterman,
Mary 44
Waters,
Anne 72
Watkins,
Ann 61
Watlington,
Leah 72
Watson,
Ann 36
Annis 69
Watts,
Mary 41
Weatheradge,
Sarah 21

Webb,
Hannah 36
Joice 69
Weldon,
Ruth 26
Wells,
Elizabeth 73
West,
Mary 17
Wha----,
Ann 12
Whiddon,
Ann 31,52
Elizabeth 18
Mary 8
Rebecca 21
White,
Amy 10
Frances 49
Juliet 75
Lydia 70
Polly 46
Prudence 55
Whitehurst,
Betty 1
Charity 57
Wigley,
Elizabeth 66
Wildair,
Elizabeth 76
Sarah 9,41,64
Wilder,
Anne 38
Mary 59
Sally 16
Wiles,
Fanny 44
Wilkins,
Agness 39
Elizabeth 55
Grace 21
Nancy 65
Sarah 50
Williams,
Anne 30,66
Dinah 22,56
Elizabeth 5,23,43
Lorana 49
Lucretia 7
Martha 49
Mary 40
Monica 20
Peggy 29
Phebe 29,67
Sarah 21
Williamson,
Fornelia 46
Margaret 38,69
Margarett 2
Martha 48
Polly 43,63
Willie,
Sophia 13
Willis,
Dorcas 46
Mary 25
Willoughby,
Ann 6,16
Margaret 70
Martha 44,56
Mary (2) 56
Wilson,
Abby 56
Alice 55
Anne 49
Elizabeth 29,33,61,63
Esther 63
Euphan 16,35
Frances 29,43
Grace 18
Hannah 30
Jane 74
Margaret 32,61,73

```
Wilson, cont'd.
     Mary      6,7,34,39,45,74
     Mason               68
     Nancy               30
     Polly               38
     Prudence      61,63,72
     Sarah            14,24
     Tabitha             25
Wise,
     Ann                 42
Wishart,
     Anne                64
     Mary                 4
Wittingham,
     Elizabeth           30
Wonycott,
     Ann                 53
     Mary                40
     Rebecca             58
Wood,
     Dinah               23
     Martha              66
Woodside,
     Elizabeth           71
Wooldridge,
     Ruth                61
Wormington,
     Mary                74
Wormsley,
     Ann                 55
Wray,
     Molly               53
Wright,
     Ann                 53
     Anne             41,63
     Elisabeth           64
     Mary      1,32,43,60
     Patience            53
     Sarah               41
Wrighting,
     Elizabeth           34
Writin,
     Elizabeth           71
Wyatt,
     Patty               43
Wyllie,
     Frances             47


              Y

Yewill,
     Sarah               40
Young,
     Peggy               22


          *  *  *
```

www.ingramcontent.com/pod-product-compliance
Lightning Source LLC
Chambersburg PA
CBHW021837020426
42334CB00014B/677